SUPER BOWL

Super Bowl
stadium

Franco Harris

Super Bowl
VIII coin

MVP watch

Jerry Rice

Super Bowl
XXXIII pin

Emmitt Smith

Game ball

EYEWITNESS BOOKS

SUPER BOWL

Created by
NFL PUBLISHING
Written by
JAMES BUCKLEY, JR.

Pregame Show
performer

Marcus Allen

Game ball
delivery

Brett Favre

Super Bowl
III ring

Super Bowl
XXXII game
program

Denver
Broncos flag

DK
A Dorling Kindersley Book

Super Bowl
XXX pin

New York
Titans pennant

Dorling Kindersley

LONDON, NEW YORK, SYDNEY, DELHI, PARIS,
MUNICH and JOHANNESBURG

NFL PUBLISHING
Editor-in-Chief John Wiebusch
Managing Editor Chuck Garrity, Sr.
Project Art Director Bill Madrid
Project Editor James Buckley, Jr.
Director–Manufacturing Dick Falk
Director–Print Services Tina Dahl
Manager–Computer Graphics Sandy Gordon

DORLING KINDERSLEY
Publisher Neal Porter
Executive Editor Iris Rosoff
Art Director Dirk Kaufman

First American Edition, 2000
2 4 6 8 10 9 7 5 3 1

Published in the United States by
Dorling Kindersley Publishing, Inc.
95 Madison Avenue
New York, New York 10016
Copyright © 2000
Dorling Kindersley Publishing, Inc.
Text copyright © NFL Properties, Inc.

Joe Montana

Terry Bradsha

John Elway

Dorling Kindersley Publishing, Inc. offers special discounts for bulk purchases for
sales promotions or premiums. Specific, large-quantity needs can be met with
special editions, including personalized covers, excerpts of existing guides, and
corporate imprints. For more information, contact Special Markets Dept., Dorling
Kindersley Publishing, 95 Madison Ave., New York, NY 10016. Fax: 800-600-9098.

Library of Congress Cataloging-in-Publication Data

Buckley, James, Jr.
    Super Bowl/by James Buckley, Jr.—1st American ed.
        p. cm.— (Dorling Kindersley Eyewitness)
    Includes index.
    Summary: A history of the Super Bowl, including chapters on
stadiums, television broadcasts, and notable plays.
    ISBN 0-7894-6300-8 (hardcover)
    ISBN 0-7894-6301-6 (paperback)
    ISBN 0-7894-6987-1 (library binding)
    1. Super Bowl—History—Juvenile literature. [1. Super Bowl—
History 2. Football—History.] I. Title. II. Series:

GV956.2.S8 B83 2000
796.332'648—dc21   00-020652

Printed in China.

see our complete catalog at
www.dk.com

Contents

Bart Starr

Before the Super Bowl

THE NATIONAL FOOTBALL LEAGUE was founded in 1920. Actually, it first was known as the American Professional Football Association; it became the NFL in 1922. And, like any league, it had to have a champion. From 1920 to 1932, the champion usually was the team with the best record; most often, there were no playoff games. The Akron Pros won the title in 1920. Beginning in 1933, the NFL split into Eastern and Western Divisions. The division champions played the NFL Championship Game to determine the league's overall winner. That game was played each season through 1969, when the NFL merged with the American Football League. The Super Bowl, played each January in a neutral site, then became the NFL's official championship game.

EARLY CHAMPIONSHIP TROPHY
The Cleveland Bulldogs won this trophy as the 1924 NFL champions. The Bulldogs originally played in Canton, Ohio. In 1924, the two-time defending NFL-champion club was purchased and moved to Cleveland. It disbanded after 1927. Notice the more bulbous shape of the 1920s-era ball on which this trophy was modeled.

"Sudden death" in the NFL playoffs means that the first team to score in overtime wins the game.

FOOTBALL FROM A CLASSIC GAME
This painted ball honors the 1958 title game won by Baltimore. Many teams award these painted "game balls" to outstanding players or coaches.

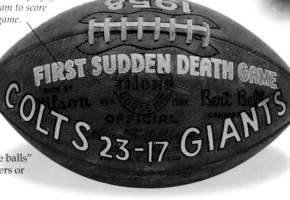

FIRST SUDDEN DEATH GAME
COLTS 23-17 GIANTS

THEN, EVERYTHING CHANGED
The NFL grew slowly throughout the 1950s. Baseball still was America's favorite sport, and college football boasted more fans than the pro game. But one particular NFL Championship Game and the manner in which many people enjoyed it, changed American sports forever. In 1958, the Baltimore Colts, led by Johnny Unitas (19), defeated the New York Giants 23-17 in the first sudden death overtime game in NFL history. The dramatic game was watched by millions on national television for the first time. The marriage between football and TV was an instant success. The game would prove to be the springboard to the Super Bowl's success in years to come.

DA BEARS
The Chicago Bears were one of the NFL's original teams, having started as the Decatur Staleys in 1920. In 1963, they won the last of their eight pre-Super Bowl NFL titles. This commemorative ball carries the signatures of the entire team.

Signature of Hall of Fame defensive lineman Doug Atkins

COVERED IN GLORY
These program covers are from NFL Championship Games (1960, top, and 1949) won by the Philadelphia Eagles.

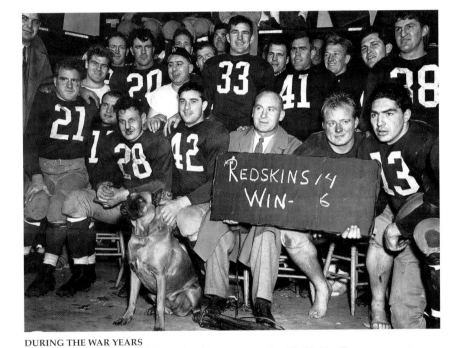

DURING THE WAR YEARS
The NFL continued to hold championship games during World War II. In 1942, the Washington Redskins (above) defeated Chicago 14-6, although the undefeated Bears were favored.

Early helmets were made of leather.

Helmets were not required until 1943.

Pads were sewn into jersey and pants

FIRST GAME
In 1933, for the first time, the NFL planned an official championship game. The Chicago Bears (lateraling ball, right) defeated the New York Giants 23-21 at Wrigley Field in Chicago.

How the Super Bowl Was Born

IN 1960, THE AMERICAN FOOTBALL LEAGUE was created to challenge the NFL. Over the years, other leagues had come and gone in an attempt to match the NFL's success. The AFL came closest with eight teams (which eventually grew to 10 teams), and an exciting, wide-open style of play that caught fans' attention. Many AFL teams, notably the San Diego Chargers and Oakland Raiders, used exciting passing games. The AFL held its own championship game from 1960 to 1969, as well as its own college draft that lured some top players away from the NFL. Recognizing that cooperation would be better than competition, the NFL and AFL began to discuss a merger between the two leagues.

AFL logo

PART OF THE "FOOLISH CLUE
Among the leaders of the new AFL were (left to right) Lama Hunt of the Dallas Texans/Kansas City Chiefs (and also AF founder), Ralph Wilson of the Buffalo Bills, Wayne Valley the Oakland Raiders, and Billy Sullivan of the New Englar Patriots. They called themselves the Foolish Clul

THE MAN WHO MADE THE SUPER BOWL
In 1960, Los Angeles Rams executive Pete Rozelle was elected NFL commissioner. He would change sports in America like few other people. Rozelle led the negotiations with the AFL that created the Super Bowl. He also recognized the importance of television to the NFL's future.

TWO LEAGUE
The AFL used th logo at top le when the leagu was first formed The NFL used th bottom logo fc many years unt modifying it slightl in 1981. After th merger, the AFL team joined the NFL which was spl into the America and Nationa Conferences. Th Baltimore Colts Cleveland Browns and Pittsburg Steelers moved t the new AFC t give eac conference 13 teams

SEPARATE TITLES
The two leagues held separate title games throughout the 1960s. In 1967, the Oakland Raiders (left) won the AFL title game and later lost to Green Bay in Super Bowl II. The Packers (right) won five NFL titles in the decade: 1961-62 and 1965-67. The Packers have more NFL championships (12) than any other team.

Paul Hornung (5) set an NFL record by scoring 176 points in 1960.

CKED HOUSE
is photograph of a sold-out kland Coliseum monstrates the real allenge the AFL posed the NFL. Fans were cking to many of AFL stadiums to joy top-quality, h-flying otball action. e competition players eatened the ancial health of th leagues, ding to secret erger talks tween NFL and L leaders that gan in 1966.

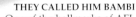

ON THE WAY TO THE FIRST SUPER BOWL
Green Bay defeated Dallas in the 1966 NFL Championship Game and earned the right to represent the NFL in the first AFL-NFL Championship Game.

The Titans'—later the Jets— original colors were blue and gold.

THEY CALLED HIM BAMBI
One of the hallmarks of AFL football was spectacular passing plays. And no one made more of them than San Diego's Lance Alworth (19), shown here in the 1963 AFL Championship Game won by San Diego. Nicknamed Bambi for his graceful gait and bounding leaps, Alworth helped create today's modern downfield passing attacks. In 1978, he became the first AFL player elected to the Pro Football Hall of Fame.

TWO ORIGINALS
The Boston Patriots (helmet, above) were an original AFL team. In 1971, the team became the New England Patriots. In 1963, another original AFL team, the Titans (pennant, above), became the New York Jets.

Super Bowl I

THE SUPER BOWL WAS BORN JUNE 8, 1966. Or, more accurately, on that day, NFL Commissioner Pete Rozelle announced the creation of the game that would become known as the Super Bowl. When the merger between the NFL and the AFL was announced, the two leagues agreed that their champions would meet in the postseason "AFL-NFL World Championship Game" to determine an overall champion. Following the 1966 season, the Kansas City Chiefs of the AFL and the Green Bay Packers of the NFL met on January 15, 1967. For the only time in Super Bowl history, the game was not a sellout. There were more than 30,000 empty seats in the Los Angeles Memorial Coliseum as 61,946 people witnessed a 35-10 victory by Green Bay...and the start of something really big.

WEIGHTY MATTERS
As with many things associated with the first Super Bowl, the game program has become a major collectible. The cover featured a close-u[p] of a sculpture of a football player created b[y] Jean Isaacson. The cove[r] price was $1.

HE SHOWED THEM THE WAY
Green Bay coach Vince Lombardi was a star college player at Fordham, an assistant for the New York Giants in the 1950s, and the man who crafted one of football's greatest dynasties in Green Bay. Under Lombardi, the Packers won five NFL championships in seven seasons (1961-67).

SYMBOL OF VICTORY
The Packers were the fir[st] team to earn this most-coveted sign of NF[L] greatness: a Super Bowl ring. Green Bay's ring fo[r] Super Bowl I was made out of sterling silver and sported a single diamon[d] in the crown.

Chiefs' coach Hank Stram had his playe[rs] use this unique form[in] the huddle.

MARVELOUS MAX
Little-used receiver Max McGee was the unlikely star of Super Bowl I. Filling in for injured starter Boyd Dowler, McGee came off the bench to catch 2 touchdown passes from most valuable player Bart Starr (opposite, top left). In the third quarter, McGee made this juggling catch for a 13-yard touchdown.

ROCKET MAN!
In 1967, man had not yet landed on the moon, but space travel was all the rage. A unique bit of entertainment at Super Bowl I was the appearance of two men wearing rocket-propelled backpacks. They floated in over the rim of the stadium before settling down on the field before the game.

I GOT IT!
Although the Chiefs bottled up Green Bay receiver Carroll Dale on this play, they could not stop the powerful Packers' offense. Green Bay scored touchdowns in every quarter. It outgained Kansas City in total yards, 361 to 239.

KANSAS CITY, HERE THEY COME
The Chiefs were the first team to try to show that the upstart AFL was just as good as the long-established NFL. But they were not up to the task. Green Bay held Kansas City to only 1 touchdown and 1 field goal.

ALL PATCHED UP
This commemorative patch (made after the name "Super Bowl" first was officially used prior to the third AFL-NFL matchup) shows both the AFL and NFL logos.

HIT IT!
The pregame and halftime entertainment at the first Super Bowl pales in comparison to today's extravaganzas. New Orleans jazz trumpeter Al Hirt (right) played the National Anthem. The halftime show featured two college marching bands.

Super Bowls II, III, IV

Reporters covering Super Bowl II got a box lunch in this commemorative container.

GREEN BAY CONTINUED THE NFL'S DOMINANCE by defeating Oakland in Super Bowl II. The rival AFL teams had been thoroughly beaten in the first two Super Bowls. But in Super Bowl III, the unthinkable happened: The AFL defeated the mighty NFL. And the best part was that a brash young quarterback named Joe Namath had "guaranteed" the victory before the game. Namath's prediction—and the dramatic way he made it stand up—rocketed the Super Bowl onto the national sports map. The video image of Namath running off the field—waving his index finger to show who was number one—remains one of football's most memorable moments. With an NFL victory no longer a foregone conclusion, the Super Bowl quickly moved to the top of the sports scene, taking the first steps on the road to the dominant position it holds today.

SUPER BOWL II
Orange Bowl, Miami
GREEN BAY 33, OAKLAND 14

SUPER BOWL III
Orange Bowl, Miami
N.Y. JETS 16, BALTIMORE 7

SUPER BOWL IV
Tulane Stadium, New Orleans
KANSAS CITY 23, MINNESOTA 7

MAD BOMBER
Quarterback Daryle Lamonica of the Oakland Raiders led one of the most explosive offenses in football. But the Raiders couldn't solve the Packers' defense in Super Bowl II.

VITAL VICTORY
The Jets were 18-point underdogs to the mighty Baltimore Colts in Super Bowl III, but Joe Namath engineered a shocking 16-7 upset whose importance still resonates today. Namath was named the game's most valuable player.

Namath was as famous for his personality—and his trademark white football cleats—as for his talent.

A JOYFUL RIDE
Coach Vince Lombardi called riding on his players' shoulders "the best way to leave the field." After defeating Oakland in Super Bowl II, Lombardi enjoyed his final ride off the field. Soon after the game, he retired from coaching the Packers. He would go on to coach Washington for one season before dying of cancer in 1970.

SURPRISE HEROES
This pin heralds the Jets, who were the first AFL team to win the Super Bowl.

WORLD CHAMPS
JETS
NEW YORK JETS

JOHNNY U
Not even future Pro Football Hall of Fame member Johnny Unitas (19) could save the Colts in Super Bowl III. The veteran Unitas came off the bench to lead the Colts to their only score.

UNSCHEDULED LANDING
Before Super Bowl IV, pregame entertainment included a pair of hot-air balloons, one representing each team. However, the Vikings' balloon (right) foreshadowed Minnesota's fate in the game. The balloon crash-landed amid the spectators, draping its fading canopy over hundreds of people. There were no injuries, except perhaps the pilot's pride.

Patch commemorating Super Bowl III

FROM NORWAY TO CANTON
Kansas City kicker Jan Stenerud, a native of Norway, kicked 3 field goals in the Chiefs' 23-7 victory over Minnesota in Super Bowl IV. Stenerud later became the first kicker elected to the Hall of Fame.

A PAIR OF STARS
Two veteran AFL players who had been part of Kansas City's Super Bowl I losing team enjoyed great days at Super Bowl IV. Receiver Otis Taylor (89) caught a 46-yard touchdown pass from Len Dawson, the game's MVP, while running back Mike Garrett (21) scored on a 5-yard run.

Kicking tee, used on kickoffs

THINGS CHANGE
Tickets for Super Bowl IV sold for $15. Some tickets to Super Bowl XXXIV, thirty years later, went for almost $400.

13

Super Bowls V, VI, VII

SUPER BOWL V AFTER THE 1970 SEASON was the first between the American Football Conference and the National Football Conference. Meanwhile, the popularity of the Super Bowl continued to grow. Although the first Super Bowl was not a sellout, every one that followed was a huge success. In only its fifth season, the game had become one of the most watched television programs of the year. In January, 1971, the Colts and Cowboys played the first game decided in the final seconds. Two years later, a Super Bowl victory gave one team the first perfect season in NFL history.

SUPER BOWL V
Orange Bowl, Miami
BALTIMORE 16, DALLAS 13

SUPER BOWL VI
Tulane Stadium, New Orleans
DALLAS 24, MIAMI 3

SUPER BOWL VII
Memorial Coliseum, Los Angeles
MIAMI 14, WASHINGTON 7

FIRST THE KICK, THEN THE LEAP
With this 32-yard field goal (above), Colts kicker Jim O'Brien (leaping, right) gave Baltimore a 16-13 victory over Dallas in Super Bowl V. The kick came with five seconds remaining in the game, the latest winning score in Super Bowl history. O'Brien, a rookie, was so nervous before the kick he tried to pull up blades of grass to check the wind. One problem: The game was played on artificial turf.

Square-toed kicking shoe

SO CLOSE, YET SO FAR
Dallas Cowboys cornerback Mel Renfro demonstrates the reaction of the losing team in Super Bowl V. The Cowboys fell just short of the Colts. But Dallas would wait only a year to change disappointment to joy.

Patch made for Super Bowl VI showing host city

THEY WERE PERFECT
he Miami Dolphins completed the
only perfect season (17-0) in NFL
history with a 14-7 victory over
Washington in Super Bowl VII.
afety Jake Scott (right) intercepted
passes and was named the game's
most valuable player.

NK!
uising running back Larry Csonka
Miami played a big role in the
lphins' march to perfection. In
per Bowl VII, he was the leading
sher, with 112 yards on 15 carries.

THE DODGER
Dallas quarterback Roger
Staubach was the most
valuable player of the
Cowboys' Super Bowl VI
victory. Staubach's
terrific
scrambling
ability
earned him
the
nickname
"Roger the
Dodger."

HE MADE UP FOR IT
Don Shula was the
coach of the Colts' team
that lost Super Bowl III.
In 1972, he led the
Dolphins to a perfect
season. He later became
the NFL's all-time
winningest
coach.

*Commemorative medal
struck for Dolphins'
Super Bowl VII victory.*

*Players use
eye black to
lessen glare
from the sun.*

ON TOP OF THE WORLD
Coach Tom Landry of the Cowboys rides on the shoulders of his team
after Dallas won Super Bowl VI. Landry led the Cowboys from
1960-1988, taking them to five Super Bowls and winning two.

A "KIICK" OUT OF IT
Running back Jim Kiick and
the Dolphins lost to Dallas in
Super Bowl VI, but had their
revenge the next season,
winning Super Bowl VII.

Super Bowls VIII, IX, X

Linebacker Bob Matheson's jersey number gave Miami's "53" defense its name.

AFTER ANOTHER VICTORY BY MIAMI, Pittsburgh made it four in a row for the AFC with wins in Super Bowls IX and X. The old NFL (or even NFC) dominance was truly finished, and the AFC was on the rise. From 1973-1981 (Super Bowls VII to XV), only Dallas would manage a victory in Super Bowl XII. But before that could happen, in 1976 America turned 200 years old and the Super Bowl turned 10. The game began to grow in popularity internationally, becoming one of the world's most popular single-day sporting events. The circus atmosphere and intense media attention were on an upward growth curve that continues today.

SUPER BOWL VIII
Rice Stadium, Houston
MIAMI 24, MINNESOTA 7

SUPER BOWL IX
Tulane Stadium, New Orleans
PITTSBURGH 16, MINNESOTA 6

SUPER BOWL X
Orange Bowl, Miami
PITTSBURGH 21, DALLAS 17

Super Bowl VIII medallion

MOST VALUABLE POUNDER
A year after its undefeated 1972 season, Miami returned to the Super Bowl to defend its NFL title. Running back Larry Csonka was the team's workhorse in Super Bowl VIII, running for a record 145 yards, including 5- and 2-yard touchdown runs. He was named the most valuable player of the Dolphins' convincing 24-7 victory over Minnesota.

Defensive backs cover opposing receivers—or try to (right).

DOLPHINS CAN F
The Dolphins lived on t ground for the most part Super Bowl VI Quarterba Bob Grie attempt only 7 pass in the game, but completed 6, includi this one to Pa Warfield, a top receiv who would be elected the Hall of Fame in 198

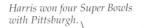
Harris won four Super Bowls with Pittsburgh.

HAPPY 200TH!
The Super Bowl X patch and program cover reflected the celebration of America's Bicentennial in 1976.

PER MOVIE
fore and during Super Bowl X,
ollywood met the NFL when scenes for
e movie *Black Sunday* were filmed. In
e movie, criminals try to disrupt the
per Bowl. Actor Robert Shaw (left)
d director John Frankenheimer
re on the sidelines before the
me...and before filming
rted.

FRANCO!
After winning MVP honors in Super Bowl IX, Pittsburgh running back Franco Harris had another good day in Super Bowl X, helping the Steelers defeat Dallas 21-17.

SUPER SWANN
Pittsburgh receiver Lynn Swann put on a show in Super Bowl X that still is regarded as one of the best days ever for a player in a Super Bowl. He had 4 spectacular catches for 161 yards and 1 touchdown. Swann, the game's MVP, made one catch (right) while falling sideways over a Dallas defender. His 64-yard touchdown catch proved to be the winning points.

THE STEEL CURTAIN
The key to the Pittsburgh Steelers' victory in Super Bowl IX was its powerful defense, nicknamed the "Steel Curtain," that held Minnesota to a record-low 17 rushing yards.

Super Bowls XI, XII, XIII

By the mid-1970s, the Super Bowl had become bigger than ever. During the three games on these pages, records were set for attendance and television audience. More than 103,000 people filled Pasadena's Rose Bowl for Super Bowl XI, and more than 102 million fans watched Super Bowl XII. During this three-year span, a former AFL team (the Raiders) won the first of its three championships, Dallas's Doomsday Defense made its name, and Pittsburgh's AFC dynasty continued its dominance with the third of its four Super Bowl victories in six years.

*Vikings' masco[...]
from 1970s*

MAN IN BLACK AND SILVER
Receiver Fred Biletnikoff combined grace, great hands, and the Oakland Raiders' legendary toughness. Biletnikoff was the most valuable player of Oakland's 32-14 victory in Super Bowl XI, the first of three NFL titles the former AFL franchise would earn.

FRAN THE MAN
When Fran Tarkenton retired in 1978, he was the NFL's all-time leader in attempts, completions, and touchdown passes. Unfortunately, he also was 0-3 in Super Bowls, including a loss in XI.

MAD ABOUT MADDEN
Head coach John Madden won 73 percent of his games in 10 seasons as the Raiders' head coach, including Oakland's victory over Minnesota in Super Bowl XI.

YES, THEY WE[...]
Gene Upshaw told the footb[...] world what the Raiders h[...] become after Super Bo[...] XI. In 1987, Upsh[...] was elected to [...] Pro Football H[...] of Fam[...]

Sign provided by fan after game.

Laces wrapped with athletic tape for tighter fit.

[PA]RTY TOWN!

[N]ew Orleans, Louisiana, hosted four of the first [do]zen Super Bowls. Part of the city's appeal for [fa]ns coming to the games was its great tradition [of] jazz which enlivened everything from pregame [pa]rties to postgame parades.

SUPER MUG

Fans at Super Bowls filled their homes with souvenirs from the big game, such as this mug showing the two teams' helmets, the site, and date of the game.

SACKED!

Harvey Martin demonstrates what the Cowboys did to Denver and quarterback Craig Morton in Super Bowl XII. Co-most valuable player's Martin and Randy White led Dallas to a 27-10 victory.

Helmet with chinstrap

Wristband

[G]OLDEN ARM

[Ri]fle-armed quarterback [Te]rry Bradshaw led the [St]eelers to victory in Super [B]owl XIII. Pittsburgh [de]feated Dallas 35-31 to [be]come the first team to [w]in three Super Bowls. [B]radshaw completed 17 [of] 30 passes for 318 [ya]rds and 4 [to]uchdowns, the [mo]st a Super Bowl [re]cord. He was [na]med the [mo]st [va]luable [pl]ayer of [th]e game.

TWO SUPER PAIRS OF HANDS

Pittsburgh receivers John Stallworth (left) and Lynn Swann were formidable weapons in Super Bowl XIII. Stallworth caught 2 touchdowns in the game, including a record 75-yard score. Swann caught an 18-yard touchdown pass.

EYES ON THE PRIZE

This fan shows just how outsized and outlandish Super Bowl souvenirs can be. Of course, Dallas fans could get a Cowboys' version of the same thing.

ORANGE TURNED YELLOW

Miami's Orange Bowl was the site of Super Bowl XIII. Workers used special equipment to paint one end zone yellow for Pittsburgh of the AFC.

AFC logo painted on one end zone. The NFC logo was on the other end zone.

Super Bowls XIV, XV, XVI

A giant yellow ribbon on the Superdome welcomed home the hostages from Iran.

THE STEELERS MADE IT FOUR VICTORIES in six years in Super Bowl XIV. When Super Bowl XV rolled around a year later, the concerns of the "real" world made an impact on the game as never before. Fifty-two Americans had been held hostage in Iran for more than a year. The hostages were freed only days before the game in January, 1981. Their release added an extra sense of celebration to the Super Bowl. In Super Bowl XVI, San Francisco started a Super Bowl dynasty that would rival the Steelers for sustained excellence. Forty-Niners quarterback Joe Montana would become one of the Super Bowl's biggest stars.

SUPER BOWL XIV
Rose Bowl, Pasadena
PITTSBURGH 31, L.A. RAMS 19

SUPER BOWL XV
Superdome, New Orleans
OAKLAND 27, PHILADELPHIA 10

SUPER BOWL XVI
Silverdome, Pontiac, Michigan
SAN FRAN. 26, CINCINNATI 21

THE GO-AHEAD SCORE
John Stallworth (82) caught this 73-yard touchdown pass from MVP Terry Bradshaw to put the Steelers ahead for good in their Super Bowl XIV victory over the Los Angeles Rams.

THE TERRIBLE TOWEL
Before Super Bowl XIV, the symbol of Pittsburgh's faithful fans was unveiled in massive size. Steelers fans waved smaller versions of the yellow "Terrible Towels" to encourage their team to victory.

RAM TOUGH
Quarterback Vince Ferragamo led the Rams to their first Super Bowl appearance.

MARTIN-IZED
In Super Bowl XV, linebacker Rod Martin played the game of his life. He intercepted a Super Bowl-record 3 passes by Philadelphia quarterback Ron Jaworski, helping the Raiders to a 27-10 victory. "Balls just kept dropping into my lap," Martin said after the game.

SURPRISE STAR
Raiders quarterback Jim Plunkett was a backup when the 1980 season started, two years removed from being cut by San Francisco. When the season ended, he was the Super Bowl MVP.

SPECIAL PIN
At each Super Bowl, members of the media receive special lapel pins used for identification; the pins also make a valuable souvenir.

TWO TDs
Speedy Cliff Branch was a favorite target of Plunkett's passes in Super Bowl XV. Branch made 5 catches in the game, including this one, a 29-yard touchdown in the third quarter. He also caught a 2-yard touchdown pass.

Bengals running back Charles Alexander stopped short of the goal line on third down by Dan Bunz (57).

SUPER JOE, PART I
San Francisco's Joe Montana accounted for 2 touchdowns, leading the 49ers' offense flawlessly and winning his first MVP award.

Goal line

THE MOTOR CITY
Super Bowl XVI was held in Pontiac, Michigan, on the outskirts of Detroit. The cover of the Super Bowl program featured depictions of automobile hood ornaments. Detroit is famous for its auto factories.

GOAL-LINE STAND
In a key series in the third quarter, the 49ers stopped the Bengals from reaching the end zone three times from the 1-yard line. It was the turning point in the 49ers' 26-21 victory.

FROZEN FOOTBALL
Super Bowl XVI was the first Super Bowl held in a northern city. There was no snow in the Silverdome, but outside it was cold enough for this ice sculpture.

Super Bowls XVII, XVIII, XIX

By THE MID-1980S, A PATTERN WAS EMERGING around the Super Bowl. Each year, the game got bigger and more popular, and each year, different story lines were written to draw even more attention to the game. The story lines for this trio of games were as follows:

Before Super Bowl XVII, the story was Washington's "Hogs" offensive line against Miami's "Killer Bees" defense (the Hogs won).

Before Super Bowl XVIII, fans and reporters wondered whether the Raiders' attacking defense could shut down the Redskins' record-setting offense (they could). And in Super Bowl XIX, would Super Bowl XVI hero Joe Montana be replaced by young, record-setting superstar Dan Marino of the Dolphins (no, he wouldn't)? And so the stories of the Super Bowl continued.

SUPER JOE, PART II
In Super Bowl XIX, Joe Montana continued his march toward Super Bowl greatness. He passed for 3 touchdowns and a record 331 yards, and he scored on a 6-yard run. He became only the third player to win two MVP awards, joining Bart Starr and Terry Bradshaw.

Washington's receivers called themselves "The Fun Bunch," an celebrated touchdowns with this leaping group high-five.

SUPER BOWL XVII
Rose Bowl, Pasadena
WASHINGTON 27, MIAMI 17

SUPER BOWL XVIII
Tampa Stadium, Tampa
L.A. RAIDERS 38, WASHINGTON 9

SUPER BOWL XIX
Stanford Stadium, Stanford, California
SAN FRANCISCO 38, MIAMI 16

As the designated "home" team, the 49ers wore their red home jersesys.

IN THE AIR AND ON THE GROUND
Running back Roger Craig was perfect for San Francisco's multifaceted attack. In Super Bowl XIX, he scored a record 3 touchdowns, including on pass receptions and 1 on a 2-yard run.

"RIGGO" RUNS
In the fourth quarter of Super Bowl XVII, with the Redskins trailing 17-13, Redskins running back John Riggins scored on a stirring 43-yard run to give Washington the lead. Riggins, the MVP, ran for a record 166 yards in the game.

TOUCHDOWN CATCH
Washington receiver Alvin Garrett caught this pass from Joe Theismann for a 4-yard touchdown. The Redskins won their first NFL championship since 1942.

Marino was renowned for his quick release on passes.

MARCUS WAS THE MAN
Super Bowl XVIII MVP Marcus Allen made one of the Super Bowl's greatest plays—a field-crossing, cutback, 74-yard touchdown run on the final play of the third quarter.

48 WAS NOT ENOUGH
In 1984, Dan Marino set NFL records with 48 touchdown passes and 5,084 yards. But the 49ers' defense shut down Marino in Super Bowl XIX.

KY-HIGH GUY
aiders punter Ray Guy ade an important play rly in Super Bowl XVIII, aping to snag this high ap. He landed and got f a 42-yard punt, dding to his reputation perhaps the greatest FL punter ever.

FISH MEETS "MAN"
Before Super Bowl XIX, the two opposing team mascots known as "Huddles" shook hands. Or at least fins.

SUPER VIEW
The tickets for Super Bowl XIX featured the Golden Gate Bridge, located in San Francisco, California.

Super Bowls XX, XXI, XXII

As THE SUPER BOWL TURNED 20, it turned a new page in popularity, thanks to a song called "Super Bowl Shuffle." In 1985, the Chicago Bears had one of the most dominant teams in NFL history, with a powerful defense and a multifaceted offense. After 12 games they had recorded the song that would become their trademark. And, thanks mostly to a free-spirited style of play, they were enormously popular. They also had a player who would become an international superstar as much for his girth as his talent. William Perry, known from Chicago to London as "The Fridge," helped galvanize attention on the Super Bowl as few other players ever had. The game, already a national obsession, grew even bigger. Super Bowl XX became the most-watched television program in history, with more than 127 million people tuning in. *We're not here to make no trouble/We're just here to do the Super Bowl Shuffle!*

SUPER BOWL XX
Superdome, New Orleans
CHICAGO 46, NEW ENGLAND 10
SUPER BOWL XXI
Rose Bowl, Pasadena
N.Y. GIANTS 39, DENVER 20
SUPER BOWL XXII
Jack Murphy Stadium, San Diego
WASHINGTON 42, DENVER 10

THE FRIDGE
There had been Super Bowl heroes before, from Namath to Montana. But there had never been a Super Bowl folk hero until William (The Refrigerator) Perry stomped into America's living rooms. Perry, a 300-pound defensive tackle, scored on a 1-yard run in Super Bowl XX, making him one of football's unlikeliest heroes.

Fans of "Da Bears"

SWEETNESS
Running back Walter Payton (34) of the Chicago Bears was nicknamed "Sweetness" for his silky (yet solid) style as well as his personal grace. In Super Bowl XX, he helped the Bears to a 46-10 victory over New England. Payton retired in 1987 as the NFL's all-time leading runner. His tragic death from cancer in 1999 saddened the sports world.

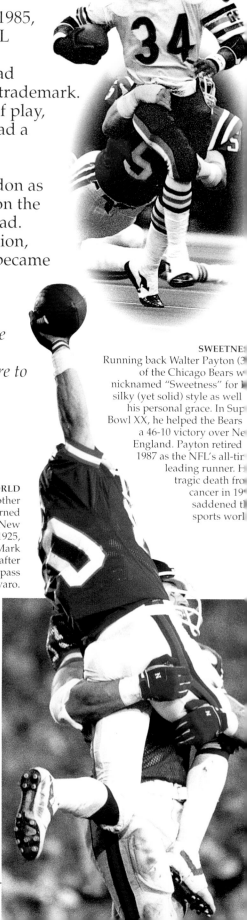

TOP OF THE WORLD
In Super Bowl XXI, another long-time NFL franchise returned to the top of the league. The New York Giants, founded in 1925, defeated Denver 39-20. Here, Mark Bavaro lifts Phil McConkey after the latter caught a touchdown pass that had bounced off Bavaro.

BACK ON TOP AGAIN
Die-hard fans of the Chicago Bears loyally stuck by their team through some very lean years in the late 1960s and 1970s. The Bears were one of the NFL's original franchises, founded in 1920. They had not won an NFL title since 1963.

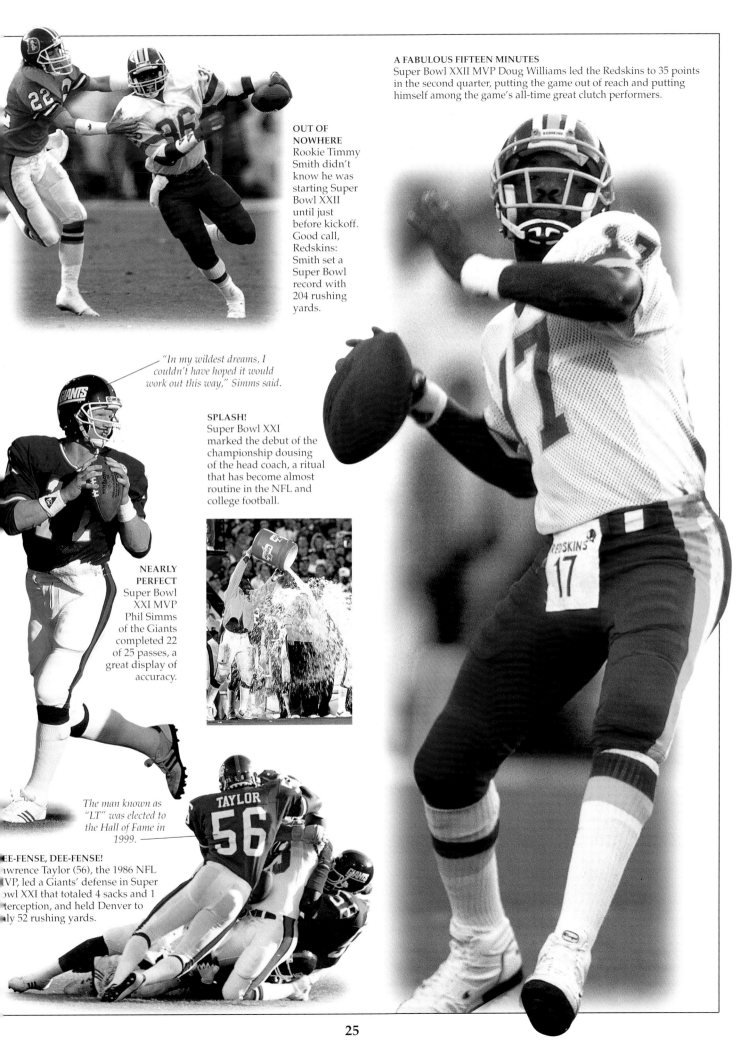

A FABULOUS FIFTEEN MINUTES
Super Bowl XXII MVP Doug Williams led the Redskins to 35 points in the second quarter, putting the game out of reach and putting himself among the game's all-time great clutch performers.

OUT OF NOWHERE
Rookie Timmy Smith didn't know he was starting Super Bowl XXII until just before kickoff. Good call, Redskins: Smith set a Super Bowl record with 204 rushing yards.

"In my wildest dreams, I couldn't have hoped it would work out this way," Simms said.

SPLASH!
Super Bowl XXI marked the debut of the championship dousing of the head coach, a ritual that has become almost routine in the NFL and college football.

NEARLY PERFECT
Super Bowl XXI MVP Phil Simms of the Giants completed 22 of 25 passes, a great display of accuracy.

The man known as "LT" was elected to the Hall of Fame in 1999.

DEE-FENSE, DEE-FENSE!
Lawrence Taylor (56), the 1986 NFL MVP, led a Giants' defense in Super Bowl XXI that totaled 4 sacks and 1 interception, and held Denver to only 52 rushing yards.

25

Super Bowls XXIII, XXIV, XXV

SUPER BOWL XXIII
Joe Robbie Stadium, Miami
SAN FRAN. 20, CINCINNATI 16

SUPER BOWL XXIV
Superdome, New Orleans
SAN FRANCISCO 55, DENVER 1[

SUPER BOWL XXV
Tampa Stadium, Tampa
N.Y. GIANTS 20, BUFFALO 19

THIS TRIO OF SUPER BOWLS HAD EVERYTHING. In successive years, fans enjoyed one of the greatest game-winning drives in NFL history in XXIII, the most dominating offensive performance in Super Bowl history in XXIV, and the combination of total joy and gut-wrenching agony that was Super Bowl XXV. The Super Bowl wrapped up its first quarter-century with games that featured superstars (Joe Montana and Jerry Rice) doing what they do best, and with a missed field goal that forever made the words "wide right" a meaningful part of the NFL vocabulary Super Bowl XXV was decided when Buffalo's Scott Norwood missed a 47-yard field-goal attempt—wide right. But to Bills' fans credit, they greeted Norwood with a standing ovation at a city ceremony.

THE ARCHITECT
Innovative coach Bill Walsh led the 49ers to their first three Super Bowl victories.

DOMINATION
The 49ers' offense completely controlled Super Bowl XXIV, outgaining Denver in total yards (461 to 167) and setting a record with 55 points.

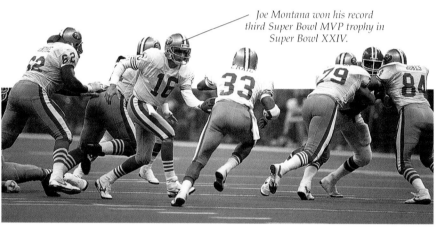

Joe Montana won his record third Super Bowl MVP trophy in Super Bowl XXIV.

Patch celebrating New Orleans, home to Super Bowl XXIV

Special patch worn on both teams' uniforms

BALL CONTROL
Jeff Hostetler filled in for injured starter Phil Simms in the playoffs. In Super Bowl XXV, Hostetler led a Giants' offense that controlled the ball for more than 40 minutes.

GRINDING IT OUT
In Super Bowl XXV, Giants running back Ottis Anderson was one of the keys to the Giants' game plan against high-scoring Buffalo. Anderson earned the MVP award by carrying the ball 21 times for 102 yards, and scoring on a 1-yard run. His powerful running helped the Giants keep the ball...and helped keep the Bills' offense off the field.

SPECIAL SOUVENIR
Only NFL staff and media members who had been at every Super Bowl received this special replica of the Super Bowl trophy.

HAPPY BIRTHDAY!
The Super Bowl celebrated its Silver Anniversary quietly as the party atmosphere was diluted because of the Gulf War.

RICE WAS NICE
Receiver Jerry Rice was the Super Bowl XXIII MVP after catching 11 passes for a Super Bowl-record 215 yards. Rice's 7 career Super Bowl touchdowns also are the most ever.

Rice, like many receivers, wears special gloves that give him a better grip on the ball.

AME WINNER
n Taylor (82) caught this 10-yard uchdown pass from Joe Montana th 34 seconds left in Super Bowl XIII. Montana led the 49ers to this nning score after a 92-yard drive less than three minutes.

WIDE RIGHT
Buffalo kicker Scott Norwood set off a Giants' celebration when he missed this 47-yard field-goal attempt with four seconds left that would have given Buffalo its first Super Bowl victory.

READY JUST IN CASE
ats are made for both teams to be ready for earing at the end of games. The Bills lost four per Bowls and never got to wear this cap.

THE JOY OF VICTORY
Giants cornerback Everson Walls celebrates as Norwood's kick sails wide right. The Giants' exuberant postgame celebration helped demonstrate the closely fought battle that preceded it.

MAY WE SEE YOUR PASS?
Security always is tight at Super Bowls. This pass was worn by league officials at Super Bowl XXV.

SUPER BOWL XXV

Official

Super Bowls XXVI, XXVII, XXVIII

Minneapolis's Metrodome was home to Super Bowl XXVI, northern-most game ever played

THE SUPER BOWL HAS CREATED several dynasties; that is, teams that have returned repeatedly to the championship stage. The three games on this page represent three parts of one of the most unusual dynasties, that of the Buffalo Bills. From 1990 to 1993, the Bills were the AFC champions and became the only team to reach four consecutive Super Bowls. Unfortunately, they also were the only team to lose four consecutive Super Bowls. The Bills lost close Super Bowls (XXV) and blowout Super Bowls (XXVII). They played well (XXVIII) and not so well (XXVII again). They became the only team to lose Super Bowls to the same team in consecutive years (to Dallas in XXVII and XXVIII). However, their continued effort to return year after year in the face of disappointment remains a remarkable story of achievement.

SUPER BOWL XXVI
Metrodome, Minneapolis
WASHINGTON 37, BUFFALO 24

SUPER BOWL XXVII
Rose Bowl, Pasadena
DALLAS 52, BUFFALO 17

SUPER BOWL XXVIII
Georgia Dome, Atlanta
DALLAS 30, BUFFALO 13

RYPIEN RIPPED 'EM
Washington quarterback Mark Rypien entered Super Bowl XXVI as an unheralded passer. He left as the game's most valuable player, completing 18 of 33 passes for 292 yards and 2 touchdowns. It was the Redskins' third Super Bowl title in 10 years.

Quarterbacks sometimes wear small towels to wipe their hands between plays.

MARVELOUS MONK
Redskins receiver Art Monk (81) had 7 catches for 113 yards in Super Bowl XXVI. Monk retired in 1995 as the NFL's all-time leading receiver.

The Super Bowl XXVI pin featured a magical ice palace design for the Minneapolis game.

KING OF THE COWBOYS
Troy Aikman was the number-one overall pick in the 1989 NFL draft. Four years later, he proved that Dallas had chosen wisely by leading the Cowboys to victory in Super Bowl XXVII. Aikman passed for 4 touchdowns and was named the game's MVP.

Owner Jerry Jones holds the Lombardi Trophy.

"HOW 'BOUT THEM COWBOYS?!"
That was the triumphant cry of coach Jimmy Johnson (right) after his Cowboys won their first NFL championship in 15 years by defeating Buffalo 52-17 in Super Bowl XXVII.

Buffalo helmet logo for city of Buffalo, New York

KELLY'S HEROES
Buffalo's Jim Kelly is the only quarterback to lead his team to four consecutive Super Bowl berths. His name can be found throughout the Super Bowl record book, including most completions in a game (31 in XXVIII), and the second-highest totals for career attempts and completions. But most fans will likely remember the one thing he didn't accomplish: a Super Bowl championship.

Georgia, home to Super Bowl XXVIII, is famous for its peaches.

HE SHOWED HEART
Dallas's Leon Lett (78) made a long run with a fumble recovery in XXVII and was near the goal line. But Buffalo receiver Don Beebe (82) never gave up the chase, finally knocking the ball away from Lett for a touchback.

ELECTRIC EMMITT
It is often the case that the greatest players shine brightest on the biggest stage. That was true for Dallas running back Emmitt Smith in Super Bowl XXVIII. After his team fell behind Buffalo 13-6 at halftime, Smith took over. His 2 second-half touchdowns helped the Cowboys pull away and seal their second consecutive Super Bowl victory. Smith ran for 132 yards and was the game's MVP.

Super Bowls XXIX, XXX, XXXI

SUPER BOWL XXIX
Joe Robbie Stadium, Miami
SAN FRANCISCO 49, SAN DIEGO

SUPER BOWL XXX
Sun Devil Stadium, Tempe, Arizona
DALLAS 27, PITTSBURGH 17

SUPER BOWL XXX
Superdome, New Orleans
GREEN BAY 35, NEW ENGLAND

THE NATIONAL FOOTBALL LEAGUE celebrated its 75th anniversary during the 1994 season. The league named its All-Time Team, and players wore special patches on their uniforms all season. At Super Bowl XXIX after that season, many events were held to mark the occasion. During th game itself, one of the members of the All-Time Team put a final sparklin candle on the league's birthday cake. Jerry Rice, one of four receivers on the anniversary team, caught a 44-yard touchdown pass on the game's third play. The celebration continued in the next two Super Bowls, as former champions returned to the top.

Banner heralding NFL's 75th anniversary

Numerals on NFL jerseys must be 8 inches high and 4 inches wide.

STEVE'S SILVER
San Francisco quarterback Steve Young put on a super show in Super Bowl XXIX. The lefty passed for 325 yards and a record 6 touchdowns. Why is this man smiling? He holds the Lombardi Trophy and was the game's MVP.

DANCIN WATTE
San Francis running ba Ricky Watt was one of tv 49ers to tie a Sup Bowl record with touchdowns in Sup Bowl XXIX (Jerry R was the other). Watte made 2 scoring catch and a touchdown ru

THE MAN IN CHARGE
The unseen hero of every Super Bowl since XIV is Jim Steeg, the NFL's vice president of special events. He is in charge of making every Super Bowl a successful one.

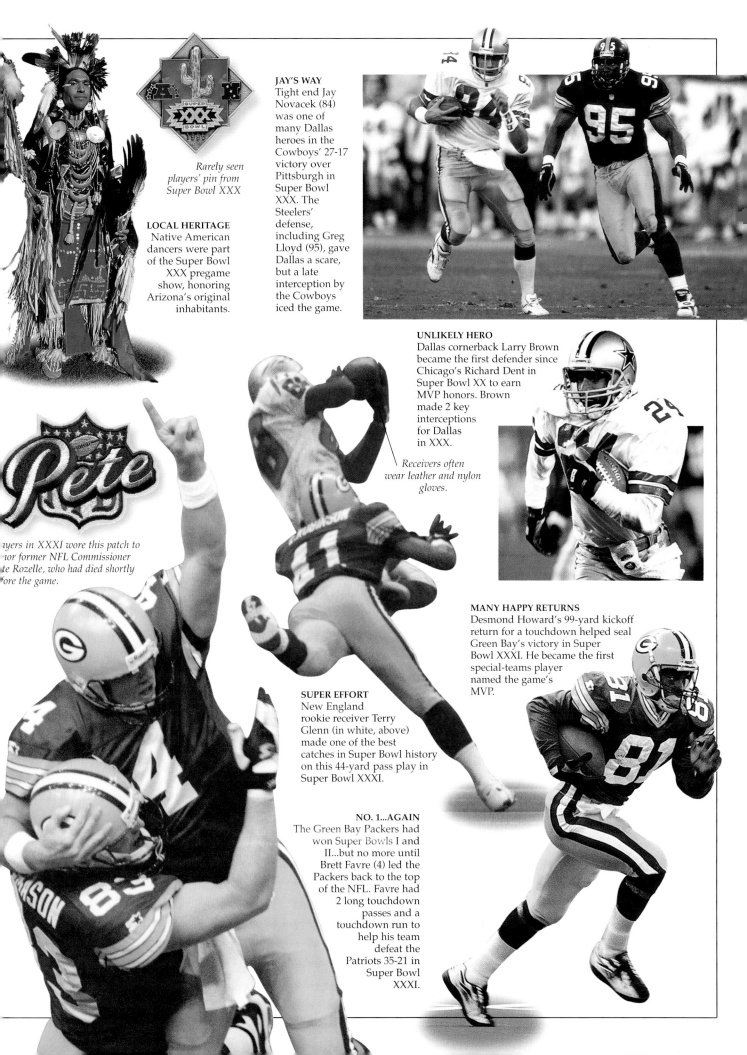

Rarely seen players' pin from Super Bowl XXX

LOCAL HERITAGE
Native American dancers were part of the Super Bowl XXX pregame show, honoring Arizona's original inhabitants.

JAY'S WAY
Tight end Jay Novacek (84) was one of many Dallas heroes in the Cowboys' 27-17 victory over Pittsburgh in Super Bowl XXX. The Steelers' defense, including Greg Lloyd (95), gave Dallas a scare, but a late interception by the Cowboys iced the game.

UNLIKELY HERO
Dallas cornerback Larry Brown became the first defender since Chicago's Richard Dent in Super Bowl XX to earn MVP honors. Brown made 2 key interceptions for Dallas in XXX.

Receivers often wear leather and nylon gloves.

...ayers in XXXI wore this patch to ...or former NFL Commissioner ...e Rozelle, who had died shortly ...ore the game.

SUPER EFFORT
New England rookie receiver Terry Glenn (in white, above) made one of the best catches in Super Bowl history on this 44-yard pass play in Super Bowl XXXI.

MANY HAPPY RETURNS
Desmond Howard's 99-yard kickoff return for a touchdown helped seal Green Bay's victory in Super Bowl XXXI. He became the first special-teams player named the game's MVP.

NO. 1...AGAIN
The Green Bay Packers had won Super Bowls I and II...but no more until Brett Favre (4) led the Packers back to the top of the NFL. Favre had 2 long touchdown passes and a touchdown run to help his team defeat the Patriots 35-21 in Super Bowl XXXI.

Super Bowls XXXII, XXXIII

SUPER BOWL XXXII
Qualcomm Stadium, San Diego
DENVER 31, GREEN BAY 24

SUPER BOWL XXXIII
Pro Player Stadium, Miami
DENVER 34, ATLANTA 19

THE 1900S EARNED THE NICKNAME, at least in the world of sports, the "NFL Century." As that century drew to a close, the Denver Broncos, led by veteran quarterback John Elway and young running back Terrell Davis, won back-to-back Super Bowl titles, neatly wrapping up a number of story lines that have wound their way through the history of the game and the league. For instance, the NFL had merged with several leagues, including the AFL, of which Denver was a part. Elway represented the many passers who have made NFL offenses so exciting in recent years. Davis was a throwback to the powerful running games that dominated early NFL play. Denver's opponents also told a story: first Green Bay, born in the 1920s, then Atlanta, born in the 1960s. With new faces and old, the Super Bowl story continues in the new century.

Denver's mascot was riding high after the team's Super Bowl wins.

THIS ONE'S FOR JOHN!
After losses in three previous Super Bowls, Denver quarterback John Elway finally knew the joy of holding up the Lombardi Trophy.

TDs FOR T.D.
Terrell Davis lived up to his initials while earning MVP honors in Super Bowl XXXII. Davis set a Super Bowl record with 3 rushing touchdowns, including the game-winner with less than two minutes remaining. His powerful running, for a total of 157 yards, was key to Denver's first NFL championship.

PACKERS SENT PACKING
Green Bay tight end Mark Chmura caught a touchdown pass, one of 3 thrown by Brett Favre, but it wasn't enough to earn the Packers their second Super Bowl title in a row.

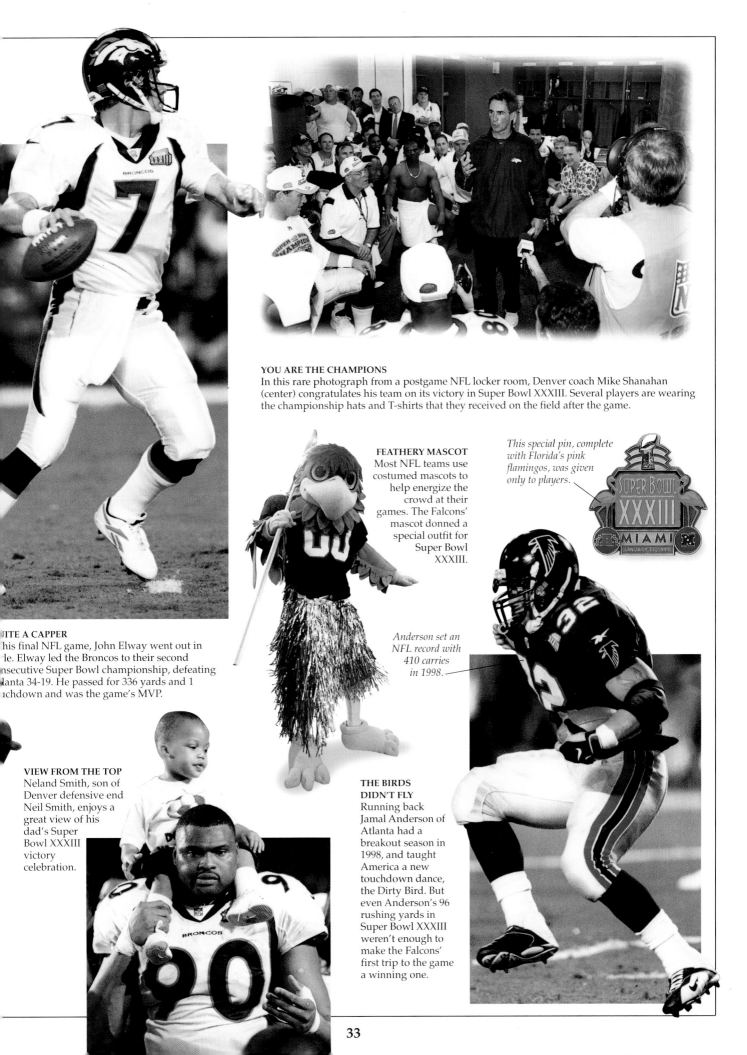

YOU ARE THE CHAMPIONS
In this rare photograph from a postgame NFL locker room, Denver coach Mike Shanahan (center) congratulates his team on its victory in Super Bowl XXXIII. Several players are wearing the championship hats and T-shirts that they received on the field after the game.

FEATHERY MASCOT
Most NFL teams use costumed mascots to help energize the crowd at their games. The Falcons' mascot donned a special outfit for Super Bowl XXXIII.

This special pin, complete with Florida's pink flamingos, was given only to players.

...ITE A CAPPER
...his final NFL game, John Elway went out in ...le. Elway led the Broncos to their second ...nsecutive Super Bowl championship, defeating ...lanta 34-19. He passed for 336 yards and 1 ...chdown and was the game's MVP.

Anderson set an NFL record with 410 carries in 1998.

VIEW FROM THE TOP
Neland Smith, son of Denver defensive end Neil Smith, enjoys a great view of his dad's Super Bowl XXXIII victory celebration.

THE BIRDS DIDN'T FLY
Running back Jamal Anderson of Atlanta had a breakout season in 1998, and taught America a new touchdown dance, the Dirty Bird. But even Anderson's 96 rushing yards in Super Bowl XXXIII weren't enough to make the Falcons' first trip to the game a winning one.

Trophies

P LAYERS JOKINGLY REFER TO TROPHIES AS "THE HARDWARE." But the players all know that to earn one of the trophies on these pages takes hard work. The most important trophy in the National Football League is the one awarded to the team that wins the Super Bowl. That trophy (left) is known as the Vince Lombardi Trophy. It is named for the legendary coach who led the Green Bay Packers to five NFL titles in the 1960s, as well as victories in the first two Super Bowls. The Lombardi Trophy is made of sterling silver, stands 21 inches high, and weighs 7 pounds. The football atop its triangular base is a regulation-size NFL ball. It was first designed by Tiffany's Oscar Reidener in 1966. But those are just facts. What is important about the Lombardi Trophy is what it means— to those who earn it and those who strive for it.

Lombardi Trophy name hand engraved on base

Applied, etched NFL shield

STEP O
These exclusive pho show the process craftsmen of Tiffany Co. go through ea year to create the Vi Lombardi Trop Here are silver she prior to silversmithi

WINNING WATCH
Until Super Bowl XXV, the most valuable player in the Super Bowl received this commemorative watch. Dallas's Chuck Howley, in Super Bowl V, was the only player from a losing team to be named MVP. Super Bowl XII had the only co-MVPs: Harvey Martin and Randy White of the Cowboys.

FOR THE AFC CHAMPION
Upon the establishment of the AFC and NFC in 1970, two new trophies were created to honor the champions of each conference. The AFC trophy is named for AFL founder and long-time Kansas City Chiefs owner Lamar Hunt. The trophy sits on a football-shaped wooden base. A silver bas-relief scene of football action is the backdrop for the brass AFC logo. A pair of plaques on the front list the name of the trophy and the champions' name and year.

STEP TWO
The larger silver sheets are spun into two ~~~nes~~ that form the football atop the base. This process takes about three days.

STEPS THREE AND FOUR
The two cones are soldered together (the tape is removed before polishing). On the right, the stitches of the ball have been applied by hand, and the seams have been "chased."

STEP FIVE
Another silver sheet is used to create the base. It is cut and shaped into three concave sections, then soldered together. Engraving is done before the football is attached. After a final polishing, the trophy is placed into a velvet-lined case and transported to the NFL for inspection. A backup trophy also is made.

DREAM COME TRUE
Hours in the weight room...days on the practice field...nights studying the playbook...and Sunday afternoons giving it all they've got. Why do NFL players do it? Simple: They do it so they can be like Reggie White (left) and the 1996 Packers and all the other Super Bowl winners. They put up with all the hard work and the sacrifice and the sweat for the chance to hold the Vince Lombardi Trophy and call themselves NFL champions.

The hand-engraved inscription includes the name of the trophy, the Super Bowl logo, and the words "most valuable player."

MVP
Since Super Bowl XXV, the most valuable player of the Super Bowl has been awarded the Pete Rozelle Trophy, also created by Tiffany & Co. It is named for the NFL's former commissioner (1960-1989) and the man most responsible for pro football's status as America's number-one sport.

FOR THE NFC CHAMPION
~~~S~~imilar in design to the AFC trophy, the NFC championship trophy is named for George ~~~H~~alas. Halas, an NFL founder and long-time ~~~o~~wner of the Chicago Bears, was the only ~~~m~~an to win NFL championships as a ~~~p~~layer, coach, and owner. He was inducted as a member of the ~~~in~~augural class of the Pro Football Hall of Fame in 1963. Two years after Halas's death in 1983, his Chicago team hoisted the trophy ~~~b~~earing his name on their way to victory in Super Bowl XX.

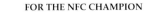

Trophy awarded to the San Francisco 49ers after their victory in the 1984 NFC Championship Game.

Super Bowl Rings

THEY PLAY FOR THE RINGS. Before Super Bowl XXXII, Broncos quarterback John Elway was asked if he would trade his individual achievements, created with years and years of hard work and effort, for a Super Bowl ring. Without hesitating, he said, "In a heartbeat." Football is a team game, but the one individual prize that every NFL player dreams of is a Super Bowl ring. Each member of the Super Bowl-winning team receives the ring, as does the coaching staff and selected members of the front-office staff. The NFL provides up to $5,000 fo each of 125 rings for the winners. As shown on these pages, the rings are reflective of their wearers: bold, strong, heavy, powerful, and glittering with th diamonds of success. Each team designs its rings, just as eac team designs its path to the day it earns them.

SUPER BOWL XXXII
January 25, 1998
Champion:
Denver Broncos

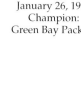

SUPER BOWL XXXI
January 26, 1997
Champion:
Green Bay Packers

SUPER BOWL XXX
January 28, 1996
Champion:
Dallas Cowboys

SUPER BOWL XXIX
January 29, 1995
Champion:
San Francisco 49ers

SUPER BOWL XXVIII
January 30, 1994
Champion:
Dallas Cowboys

FOUR FOR FOUR
San Francisco quarterback Joe Montana displays his four Super Bo rings. Montana, who also won thr Super Bowl MVP awards, is one of many players wit four rings. Defensive end Charles Haley hol the record with fi Haley played for San Francisco in Super Bowls XXII and XXIV and Dallas in Super Bowls XXVII, XXVIII, and XXX.

Most players have their rings sized to on this finger, calle the ring finger.

SUPER BOWL XXVII
January 31, 1993
Champion:
Dallas Cowboys

SUPER BOWL XXVI
January 26, 1992
Champion:
Washington Redskins

SUPER BOWL XXV
January 27, 1991
Champion:
New York Giants

SUPER BOWL XXIV
January 28, 1990
Champion:
San Francisco 49ers

SUPER BOWL XXIII
January 22, 1989
Champion:
San Francisco 49ers

SUPER BOWL XX
January 31, 1988
Champion:
Washington Redski

SUPER BOWL IV
January 11, 1970
Champion:
Kansas City Chiefs

SUPER BOWL V
January 17, 1971
Champion:
Baltimore Colts

SUPER BOWL VI
January 16, 1972
Champion:
Dallas Cowboys

SUPER BOWL VII
January 14, 1973
Champion:
Miami Dolphins

SUPER BOWL VIII
January 13, 1974
Champion:
Miami Dolphins

SUPER BOWL IX
January 12, 1975
Champion:
Pittsburgh Steelers

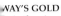

WAY'S GOLD

is is the ring that John Elway dreamed of.
d he did not have to give up his career
ords to get it. Elway and the Broncos earned
ir first rings by winning Super Bowl XXXII.
ey got rings for their other hand with a
tory in Super Bowl XXXIII. The Broncos,
e most teams, had their rings cast in
karat yellow gold, and decorated
th numerous diamonds and
er precious stones. This
per Bowl XXXIII
g was made by
tens
mpany.

*Cast in 14-karat
yellow gold; total weight
of 4.04 carats*

*Six diamonds
represent Denver's
six AFC titles*

*Orange diamonds
make up horses' manes*

*Two Broncos represent
two Super Bowl titles*

*Total of 124 diamonds
on each ring*

SUPER BOWL X
January 18, 1976
Champion:
Pittsburgh Steelers

SUPER BOWL XI
January 9, 1977
Champion:
Oakland Raiders

SUPER BOWL XII
January 15, 1978
Champion:
Dallas Cowboys

SUPER BOWL XIII
January 21, 1979
Champion:
Pittsburgh Steelers

SUPER BOWL XIV
January 20, 1980
Champion:
Pittsburgh Steelers

SUPER BOWL XV
January 25, 1981
Champion:
Oakland Raiders

SUPER BOWL XXI
January 25, 1987
Champion:
New York Giants

SUPER BOWL XX
January 26, 1986
Champion:
Chicago Bears

SUPER BOWL XIX
January 20, 1985
Champion:
San Francisco 49ers

SUPER BOWL XVIII
January 22, 1984
Champion:
Los Angeles Raiders

SUPER BOWL XVII
January 30, 1983
Champion:
Washington Redskins

SUPER BOWL XVI
January 24, 1982
Champion:
San Francisco 49ers

Amazing Super Bowl Plays

Wow, DID YOU SEE THAT? In the biggest game of all, players often come up with the biggest plays of their careers. Some of those plays are so big and so spectacular that they become a part of Super Bowl and NFL history. Of course, the importance of the Super Bowl magnifies what would be a less-important play if it occurred during the regular season. Long touchdowns runs occur nearly every week, especially by players such as Marcus Allen (right). But when that same play comes during the Super Bowl, with millions of people watching around the world, and with the NFL title at stake, the play becomes more than ordinary: It becomes extraordinary. Most of the memorable plays from Super Bowl games involve touchdowns. But two plays here involve seeming touchdowns that weren't.

PICTURE PERFECT
All players, young and old, are taught to "wrap up" the player they are tackling. Rams linebacker Mike Jones (52) wrapped up Titans receiver Kevin Dyson less than a yard short of a touchdown to preserve the Rams' Super Bowl XXXIV victory.

Allen's path to the end zone.

Marcus Allen retired after the 1998 season with 145 touchdowns, second most all-time.

ZIG-ZAG TO THE END ZONE
In Super Bowl XVIII, the Raiders' Marcus Allen made one of the best touchdown runs in Super Bowl history. Taking a handoff at the Raiders' 26-yard line, Allen first ran left—into a wall of Redskins. He reversed field and ran right, then cut back and took off up the middle. Allen dodged several tacklers and then won a sprint to the end zone. The record run helped the Raiders defeat the Redskins 38-9, and Allen was named the game's MVP.

IT'S A RUN...NO, IT'S A PASS
Sometimes the unexpected play becomes the big one. In Super Bowl XIV, Rams running back Lawrence McCutcheon (30) took a handoff and started to run. Suddenly, he stopped and threw a 24-yard touchdown pass to Ron Smith that gave the Rams a 19-17 lead over Pittsburgh. But the surprise "halfback-option" play wasn't enough; the Steelers came back to defeat the Rams.

A player who receives a handoff can then make a forward pass from behind the line of scrimmage.

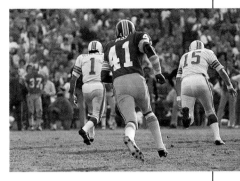

GARO'S GOOF

One of the most famous plays in Super Bowl history also was one of the goofiest. In Super Bowl VII, Miami led Washington 14-0 when Dolphins kicker Garo Yepremian (1) attempted a field goal. The kick was blocked (left), and Garo, a fine kicker but a football novice, picked the ball up and tried to pass it (center). He bobbled the ball and the Redskins' Mike Bass (41) eventually picked it up and returned it for a touchdown.

ONE THAT WASN'T

Perhaps the biggest miss in Super Bowl history came in Super Bowl XIII when Dallas tight end Jackie Smith dropped a sure touchdown catch in the third quarter of a game that Dallas lost to Pittsburgh.

Smith played 16 seasons in the NFL. He was elected to the Pro Football Hall of Fame in 1994.

HIS ONE AND ONLY

Super Bowl X was nearly over and the Cowboys trailed the Steelers 21-7. But there was enough time for Dallas receiver Percy Howard to become the answer to this trivia question: What player caught a touchdown pass in the Super Bowl for the only NFL reception of his career?

Brown had 54 interceptions in his 16-year, Hall of Fame career.

AN ASSIST FROM VIDEO

Green Bay kick returner Desmond Howard (81) had a little help as he neared the end zone during this record 99-yard kickoff-return touchdown in Super Bowl XXXI. He looked up at the giant video screen in the end zone to see how close pursuing Patriots were.

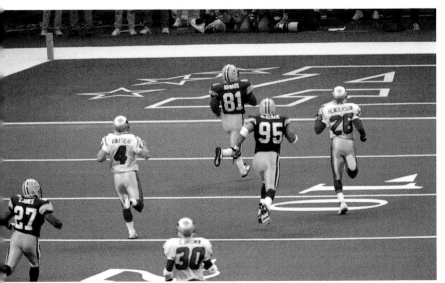

SILVER, BLACK, AND BROWN

Raiders cornerback Willie Brown set a Super Bowl record with his game-clinching 75-yard interception return for a touchdown in Super Bowl XI. The Raiders defeated the Vikings 32-14, the Raiders' first NFL championship.

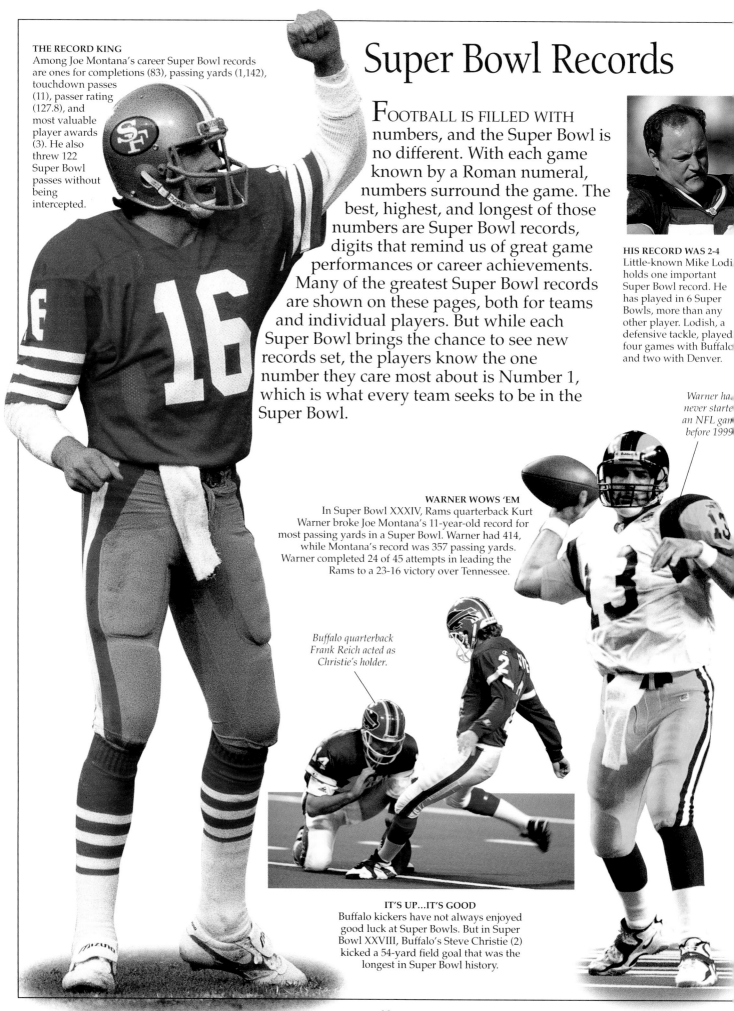

THE RECORD KING
Among Joe Montana's career Super Bowl records are ones for completions (83), passing yards (1,142), touchdown passes (11), passer rating (127.8), and most valuable player awards (3). He also threw 122 Super Bowl passes without being intercepted.

Super Bowl Records

FOOTBALL IS FILLED WITH numbers, and the Super Bowl is no different. With each game known by a Roman numeral, numbers surround the game. The best, highest, and longest of those numbers are Super Bowl records, digits that remind us of great game performances or career achievements. Many of the greatest Super Bowl records are shown on these pages, both for teams and individual players. But while each Super Bowl brings the chance to see new records set, the players know the one number they care most about is Number 1, which is what every team seeks to be in the Super Bowl.

HIS RECORD WAS 2-4
Little-known Mike Lodi holds one important Super Bowl record. He has played in 6 Super Bowls, more than any other player. Lodish, a defensive tackle, played four games with Buffalo and two with Denver.

Warner has never started an NFL game before 1999

WARNER WOWS 'EM
In Super Bowl XXXIV, Rams quarterback Kurt Warner broke Joe Montana's 11-year-old record for most passing yards in a Super Bowl. Warner had 414, while Montana's record was 357 passing yards. Warner completed 24 of 45 attempts in leading the Rams to a 23-16 victory over Tennessee.

Buffalo quarterback Frank Reich acted as Christie's holder.

IT'S UP...IT'S GOOD
Buffalo kickers have not always enjoyed good luck at Super Bowls. But in Super Bowl XXVIII, Buffalo's Steve Christie (2) kicked a 54-yard field goal that was the longest in Super Bowl history.

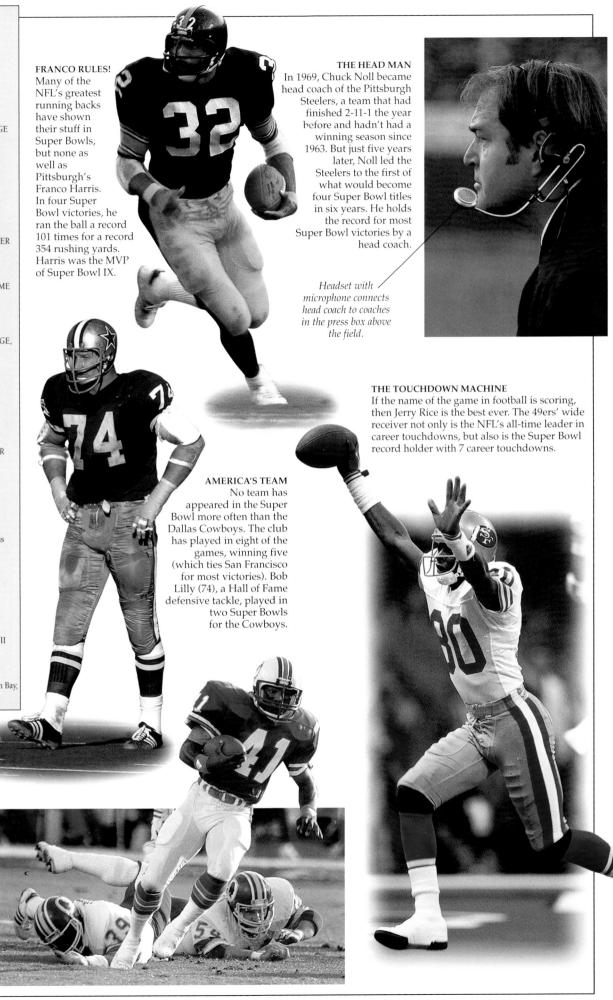

FRANCO RULES!
Many of the NFL's greatest running backs have shown their stuff in Super Bowls, but none as well as Pittsburgh's Franco Harris. In four Super Bowl victories, he ran the ball a record 101 times for a record 354 rushing yards. Harris was the MVP of Super Bowl IX.

THE HEAD MAN
In 1969, Chuck Noll became head coach of the Pittsburgh Steelers, a team that had finished 2-11-1 the year before and hadn't had a winning season since 1963. But just five years later, Noll led the Steelers to the first of what would become four Super Bowl titles in six years. He holds the record for most Super Bowl victories by a head coach.

Headset with microphone connects head coach to coaches in the press box above the field.

THE TOUCHDOWN MACHINE
If the name of the game in football is scoring, then Jerry Rice is the best ever. The 49ers' wide receiver not only is the NFL's all-time leader in career touchdowns, but also is the Super Bowl record holder with 7 career touchdowns.

AMERICA'S TEAM
No team has appeared in the Super Bowl more often than the Dallas Cowboys. The club has played in eight of the games, winning five (which ties San Francisco for most victories). Bob Lilly (74), a Hall of Fame defensive tackle, played in two Super Bowls for the Cowboys.

ALL THE WAY BACK
Some Super Bowl records involve "firsts." Sixteen Super Bowls had been played before Miami's Fulton Walker became the first player to return a kickoff for a touchdown. Walker's 98-yard return wasn't enough, however, to stop the Redskins from defeating the Dolphins in Super Bowl XVII.

Super Bowl Coaches

IF THE SUPER BOWL IS A HURRICANE OF ACTIVITY, then the head coaches are at the eye of that hurricane. During Super Week, they must not only plan for the biggest game of their careers, they must face the world's media. Head coaches take part in media sessions every day of the week, often answering the same questions many times. On Super Bowl Sunday, facing enormous pressure, the coaches call the plays, choose the players to run those plays, and then face the consequences. Once the game begins, they engage in a 60-minute chess match, with moves and countermoves. And if their plan is successful, the coaches take a joyous trip off the field on the shoulders of their players.

THE WIZARD OF WASHINGTON
Joe Gibbs was the head coach of Washington from 1981-1992, leading the Redskins to Super Bowl championships in XVII, XXII, and XXVI. Gibbs was not only a great play-caller and organizer, but a master motivator who got the most out of his players. Gibbs retired following the Redskins' third title and now is involved in auto racing.

WALSH THE WINNER
Bill Walsh led the San Francisco 49ers to Super Bowl championships in XVI, XIX, and XXIII. The team he helped create also won Super Bowl XXIV under the direction of head coach George Seifert. Walsh is regarded as one of the great offensive football minds of all time.

Walsh carefully scripted his team's first 15-20 plays each game.

THE CHIEF OF THE CHIEFS
Hank Stram not only led the Kansas City Chiefs to their only Super Bowl title, he became a permanent part of Super Bowl history. He wore a microphone during the game. His enthusiastic chatter was captured in a famous movie made by NFL Films that often is replayed at Super Bowl time.

42

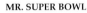

ONE BIG, BAD BEAR
Chicago Bears coach Mike Ditka was as tough as his players. His fierce style helped create the Super Bowl XX-champion Bears, one of the most dominant teams in NFL history.

MR. SUPER BOWL
Dan Reeves has participated in nine Super Bowls, more than any other person. He has taken part in Super Bowls as a player for the Dallas Cowboys, as an assistant coach for Dallas, and as head coach of the Atlanta Falcons (left) and Denver Broncos.

GOING FOR TWO
Bill Parcells (below), Dan Reeves, and Don Shula are the only coaches to lead two different teams to berths in the Super Bowl. Parcells won Super Bowls XXI and XXV with the New York Giants, using a clock-eating ground game of his design. His New England Patriots team lost Super Bowl XXXI to Green Bay.

TOM TERRIFIC
Tom Flores was the first person to earn Super Bowl rings as a player, assistant coach, and head coach. He was a backup quarterback for Kansas City (IV), an assistant for the Oakland Raiders (XI), and head coach for the Raiders in XV and XVIII. Here he rides off the field after winning Super Bowl XVIII.

CLOSE, BUT NO CIGAR
Minnesota's Bud Grant (left) and Buffalo's Marv Levy share an unfortunate distinction. Both men led their teams to four Super Bowls…and both men's teams lost four Super Bowls. Grant is in the Pro Football Hall of Fame; the recently retired Levy is now eligible, too.

Pregame Show

THE SUPER BOWL SPECTACLE DOESN'T wait for kickoff to
begin. The Pregame Show always gets the day off to an
entertaining beginning. At the first Super Bowls, the
shows weren't much more than a marching band or
some recorded music. Today, the shows are field-
spanning extravaganzas with dancers, superstar
singers and performers, fireworks, and more. Also
part of the pregame festivities are the National Anthem, the
coin toss (to determine which team kicks off and which receives), and the introduction o
the players. Each team's starting offense or defense is introduced and sprints onto the
field through a tunnel of cheerleaders and teammates. Many players call the moment
when they finally take the field for a Super Bowl one of the highlights of their careers.

DANCE, DANCE, DANCE
Every Super Bowl Pregame Show includes
hundreds of dancers, like these from XXVII.

PREGAME HIGHLIGHT
The highlight of every Pregame Show held in an
outdoor stadium always is the flyover by U.S.
military jets. Roaring overhead, the jets zoom
over the stadium at the end of the National
Anthem (as they do here at Super Bowl XXXII).
Their ear-rattling appearance always gets the gam
off to a rousing beginning.

ON THEIR FEET
For Super Bowl XXV, during the
Persian Gulf War, Whitney Houston
created a lasting memory with her
inspiring version of the National
Anthem.

OCK THE HOUSE
pular rock group KISS is one of the many
;-name stars to play during Pregame Shows.

THE ICE WAS ONLY TEMPORARY
Olympic gold medalist Brian Boitano added a unique
touch to the Pregame Show before Super Bowl XXVI in
Minneapolis by skating on a rink at the center of the field.

A SUPER BALL
Many pregame shows use enormous props,
such as these beach balls from Super
Bowl XXIX. The giant balls were
more easily seen from the stands
and made for a colorful part of
the show.

ROCKIN' THE HOUSE
Before the Rams' victory in Super
Bowl XXXIV, fans were treated to a
Pregame Show that featured rock 'n'
roll legend Tina Turner. As fireworks
exploded from cannons on the field,
Turner and country star Travis Tritt
took turns filling the Georgia Dome
with sound. Dancers covered the
field, while giant banners featuring
portraits of former Pregame
performers hung high overhead.

*Team captains often are chosen
to represent the offense,
defense, and special teams.*

HEADS OR TAILS?
The pregame coin
toss involves the
two teams'
captains, the
referee, and a
special NFL guest.
Before Super
Bowl XXVIII,
former Jets
quarterback Joe
Namath (in sport
coat) helped out.

*Special
Super
Bowl coin
used for
coin toss
ceremony*

Halftime Show

THERE ARE TWO BIG SHOWS ON Super Bowl Sunday. One begins when the game kicks off. The other begins when the first half ends. That's when the Super Bowl Halftime Show takes over while the players take a rest. In the past decade, the Halftime Show has become almost as big a part of Super Sunday as the game. Fans in the stadium and watching at home look forward to seeing some of the most popular entertainers in the world perform music ranging from pop to jazz to soul to rhythm and blues. Nothing is too big for a Halftime Show. As Diana Ross ended her performance at Super Bowl XXX, a helicopter actually landed on the stage to whisk her away, still singing, as the crowd went wild. Stay tuned...next year's show might be even wilder.

Fans sometimes perform card stunts during the show.

Acrobats swung from ropes suspended from Georgia Dome ceiling.

Giant white bird made of fabric rose behind the stage.

A THRILLER
At Super Bowl XXVII, Michael Jackson created one of the most memorable Halftime Shows, combining his energetic dancing, a thousand-voice kids' choir, and a card stunt that involved more than 100,000 people at Pasadena's Rose Bowl.

Atlanta native Toni Braxton performed in the second segment of the Super Bowl XXXIV show.

EVERYTHING BUT THE KITCHEN SIN
The Halftime Show at Super Bowl XXX included just about everything. Singer Phil Collin was the headliner, joined by singers Toni Braxto Christina Aguilera, and Enrique Iglesia The show also had giant walking puppe indoor fireworks, giant jets of flam hundreds of dancers, a 60-foot tall clo bird, and a symphony orchestr

"THE "OLD" DAYS"
Before the glitz and glamour of the Halftime Show caught up to the enormity of the game itself, the show often was as simple as cheerleaders riding on NFL helmet-covered cars, accompanied by college marching bands.

UP, UP, AND AWAY
Diana Ross boards her ride home at the conclusion of her Super Bowl XXX performance. The helicopter actually landed on the stage to whisk her away.

UP WITH SINGING
Young, peppy singing groups often have performed in Halftime Shows. Disney singers sang at Super Bowl XI (below). The group Up With People made a record four halftime appearances.

ROCKETTES AND ROCKETS
Super Bowl Halftime Shows have included everything from dancing Radio City Rockettes to real, sky-high rockets.

ROPHYNAPPERS!
e Super Bowl
IX Halftime
ow featured an
diana Jones"
aracter who
tled snakes, fire,
d bandits to
apture the Vince
mbardi Trophy.

HARD WORKING SOUL MAN
Superstar soul singer James Brown was a vision in red when he headlined the show at Super Bowl XXXI. He was joined by ZZ Top and the Blues Brothers.

The NFL Experience

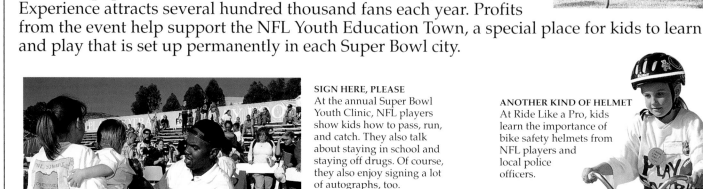

NFL LINEMAN CHALLENGE
Warren Sapp dances through the ropes at this annual Super Bowl competition among NFL linemen.

T HERE'S MORE TO THE SUPER BOWL than the game on Sunday. Each year, the Super Bowl offers fans dozens of ways to make their trip to the big game a special one. The host cities sponsor concerts, parties, festivals, and more. One of the biggest events of Super Bowl Week is The NFL Experience, a gigantic football theme park that springs to life several days before the game. Kids can play on indoor fields, try their hand at interactive football games, meet NFL players and get autographs, try on NFL equipment, and lots more. Parents can have fun, too. The NFL Experience attracts several hundred thousand fans each year. Profits from the event help support the NFL Youth Education Town, a special place for kids to learn and play that is set up permanently in each Super Bowl city.

SIGN HERE, PLEASE
At the annual Super Bowl Youth Clinic, NFL players show kids how to pass, run, and catch. They also talk about staying in school and staying off drugs. Of course, they also enjoy signing a lot of autographs, too.

ANOTHER KIND OF HELMET
At Ride Like a Pro, kids learn the importance of bike safety helmets from NFL players and local police officers.

FEET, FEET, FEET!
Kids at The NFL Experience try their hand—and feet—at games that test their football skills, such as this obstacle course race.

Padded pylons make for great obstacles at this NFL Experience event.

Padded sidewalls help keep kids safe as they run through the course.

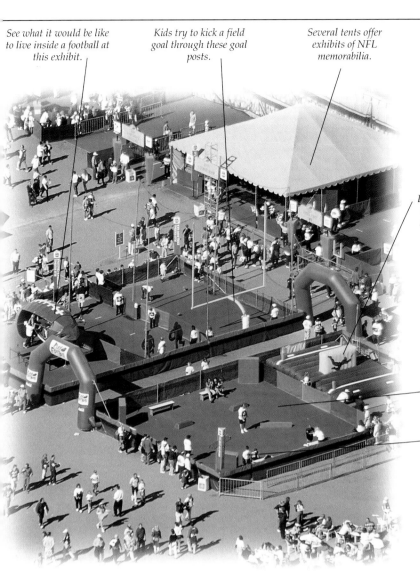

See what it would be like to live inside a football at this exhibit.

Kids try to kick a field goal through these goal posts.

Several tents offer exhibits of NFL memorabilia.

Dive over this wall onto an air-filled pad to score a touchdown.

Artificial turf is used to make several fields.

In this game, kids try to see who can put on an NFL uniform in the fastest time.

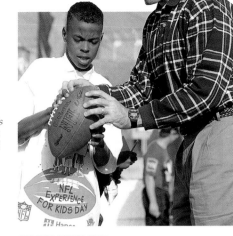

LET ME SHOW YOU
Tennessee Titans quarterback Neil O'Donnell shows a young fan how to throw a spiral. Many NFL players visit The NFL Experience.

THAT'S A BIG BEAR
Not only NFL stars visit The NFL Experience to meet fans. NFL team mascots often drop by to say hello and pose for pictures. This mascot is for the Chicago Bears.

A BIG SPREAD
The NFL Experience has been held since Super Bowl XXVI. In some cities, it is held outdoors on land near the Super Bowl stadium. In others, the event is held inside an enormous building, such as a convention center.

PUT ME IN, COACH!
Visitors can pretend they've made the team by posing inside these life-sized NFL uniforms. Uniforms from every NFL team are available for fans to "wear."

This is the symbol for NFL kids' programs.

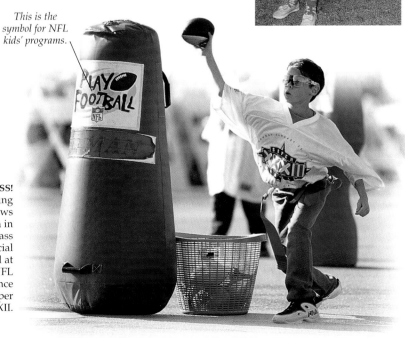

GOOD PASS!
This young player shows good form in making a pass during a special contest held at The NFL Experience before Super Bowl XXXII.

Super Bowl Collectibles

Bumper stickers for each team

Pins for the game and for each team

I F A SUPER BOWL LOGO will fit on it, you can be sure that someone will make it. What is "it"? A Super Bowl souvenir. Fans attending the game will take home football memories to last a lifetime, while fans around the world will remember watching the game on TV. But whether they go to the game or to the living room, fans are looking for more than memories to take away from the Super Bowl. That is where the souvenir and collectible makers of the world come in. Every imaginable product is available as a souvenir of the Super Bowl. These pages illustrate only a tiny fraction of the many things that fans buy to make the game part of their lives. Fans can wear the Super Bowl, eat on the Super Bowl, read the Super Bowl, decorate with the Super Bowl, play golf with the Super Bowl, and much, much more.

ON SALE HERE!
Fans in the Super Bowl host city have the best access to dozens of Super Bowl souvenirs, such as at this display at Super Bowl XXII. Some Super Bowl merchandise includes the two teams' logos; all of those items must be made in a very short time, after the teams qualify.

PIN IT ON
Metal pins (below and on following pages) are fun, easy to collect, and come in an enormous variety of styles and designs.

Pennant with teams, game, and date

Special media pin awarded to veteran Super Bowl reporters.

Super Bowl XXIV pin features Mississippi riverboat design.

Another special pin from Super Bowl XXV.

Media pin from Super Bowl XXXI features jazz musician.

Souvenir salesmen usually are local people earning extra money during Super Week.

POPULAR PROGRAM
The Official Super Bowl Game Program (right and below) always is one of the most popular collectibles available to fans. The program has stories about past games and NFL stars, as well as Super Bowl records, results from the previous season, and lineups, rosters, and scouting reports for the two Super Bowl teams.

Super Bowl XXXII Game Program

Stand set up outside stadium to sell programs.

Super Bowl XX Game Program

OTTA HAVE HATS
These hats were designed like baseball caps, but they and dozens ..e them are sold to football fans at Super Bowls. Souvenir caps are among the .ost-worn items by fans attending .uper Bowls. Many .ompanies produce .hats in a variety of .esigns and colors.

Super Bowl II Game Program

THE SILVER PAGES
NFL Publishing produced this special commemorative Super Bowl book to honor the game's 25th anniversary in 1991. The story of each game featured a gatefold illustration of action scenes of the game's heroes.

Illustration used all the NFL team helmet logos.

ABC Sports issued its own pin at Super Bowl XIX.

A pin from a set given only to veteran Super Bowl writers.

NFL sponsors make pins, too; this is from Super Bowl XX.

Super Bowl XX pin in the shape of the Lombardi Trophy.

Super Bowl Collectibles

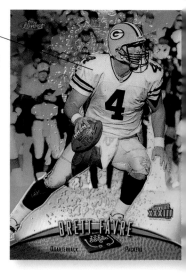

Green Bay quarterback Brett Favre

While hundreds of collectibles are available to fans, some of those items are more valuable than others. Scarcity determines a collectible's value, along with the meaningfulness of the item to the buyer. A Jets' fan, for instance, will be more interested in Super Bowl III memorabilia than the fan of another team. Special limited-edition items also rise in value over time. One of the attractions at The NFL Experience each year is the giant Super Bowl Card Show, a massive market for Super Bowl, football, and sports cards, collectibles, and, well, stuff. The Super Bowl is not only the biggest game in town… it's the biggest marketplace.

SOUVENIR PIGSKIN
The official Super Bowl football made by Wilson is stamped in gold with the game's logo. After the game, fans also can buy a ball with the score of the game stamped on it.

MORE THAN CARDBOARD
Football cards are a big hit with collectors. This Super Bowl XXXIII set used holograms to create a special look at past Super Bowl heroes.

FOR THE KIDS
Souvenirs for all ages are available at the Super Bowl. These teddy bears and squishy foam footballs are made for toddlers. T-shirts and other clothing all come in kids' sizes, too. More souvenirs have been made for children in recent seasons than in years past as the Super Bowl has grown in popularity.

FORE!
Different game, different kind of ball. Football fans took their Super Bowl memories to the golf course with this set of golf balls from Super Bowl XXI.

Pins are cast in metal from molds.

This pin was made using a process similar to cloisonne.

This Super Bowl XIX pin features the Golden Gate Bridge.

Super Bowl XXI was held at the Rose Bowl stadium.

This Super Bowl XX pin doubled as a key chain.

Super Bowl XXV got special treatment on this pin.

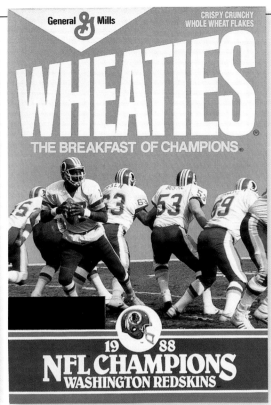

ONLY ONE WAS A WINNER

Many Super Bowl souvenirs are not sold until after the game is over, to celebrate and honor the champion. These cereal boxes were made before Super Bowl XXII, and were ready to go to stores depending on which team won. The Redskins' version was the only one that hit store shelves. The Broncos' version became a rare collectible.

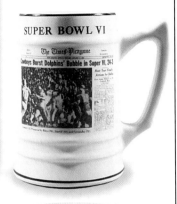

Collectors' card came with action figure.

BALLOT
SUPER BOWL XXXVI SITE

___ NEW ORLEANS
___ SAN DIEGO

CASTING A VOTE

NFL owners used cards like this one—a rarely seen piece of memorabilia—to decide what city would play host to Super Bowl XXXVI, to be played in January 2002. The winner? New Orleans, home to eight previous Super Bowls.

IT'S NOT A DOLL...

It's an action figure. These collectible figures were sold at Super Bowl XXXIII. Many of the NFL's top players were turned into moveable plastic statues.

CHEERS!

All sorts of cups, glasses, and mugs are sold at the Super Bowl, including the ceramic mugs from Super Bowl VI (top, featuring a newspaper page about the game) and Super Bowl XXIX, and the blue glass version from Super Bowl XXXIV. Fans can save them for use at next year's Super Bowl party.

The Super Bowl XIX champions were honored with this pin.

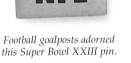

Football goalposts adorned this Super Bowl XXIII pin.

The NFLPA issued this pin for Super Bowl XX.

Miami palm trees decorated this Super Bowl XXIII pin.

The Media

ONE OF THE MOST IMPORTANT REASONS the Super Bowl has become such an enormous event is the media. Writers, reporters, photographers, cameramen, announcers, and Web site creators from around the world converge on the Super Bowl city each year by the thousands. These men and women tell the stories of the teams, the players, and the game to billions of people around the world. At Super Bowl XXXIV, more than 3,500 journalists received credentials to cover the game, sending their stories back to more than 180 countries.

Earphone connects announcer to control booth.

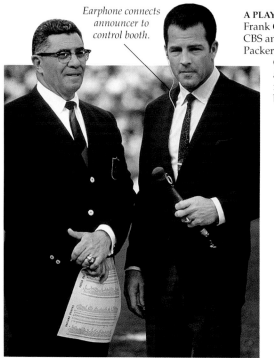

A PLAYER AND HIS FORMER COACH
Frank Gifford (with microphone, left) was one of the CBS announcers for Super Bowl I. Here he interviews Packers coach Vince Lombardi. Gifford played for the Giants in the 1950s, when Lombardi was an assistant coach with the team. Gifford is one of many former NFL players who became broadcasters after retiring.

TAKING YOU TO THE HUDDL
Television cameras help fans get right the middle of the action at Super Bowl During Super Bowl XXIII, this camerama gave fans an up-close look at the 49er pregame gathering. At Super Bowl XXXI ABC used 40 cameras to cover the gam

LOOK! UP IN THE SKY!
Several blimps fly above the Super Bowl to give TV viewers a birds-eye view of the stadium.

Pilots ride in the gondola.

SAY CHEESE!
The enormous number of press people at the game makes the postgame scene on the field quite a crowded one. Here, Packers coach Mike Holmgren rides his players' shoulders after winning Super Bowl XXXI while dozens of photographers rush in to capture the magic moment.

EVERYBODY WATCHES
Even busy world leaders take time out to watch the Super Bowl. President Bill Clinton (center) was joined by Texas Gov. Ann Richards and New York Gov. Mario Cuomo for Super Bowl XXVIII. Chelsea Clinton is sitting in front.

CROWDED HOUSE
More than 300 photographers line the sidelines of the Super Bowl, taking hundreds of thousands of photographs before, during, and after the game. Most of them use special long lenses to get deep into the action.

ACE SHOOTERS
The best sports photographers in the world cover the Super Bowl. They come to the game with several cameras and lenses and other equipment to do their job.

One of two different cameras

Light meter

Field pass

Team helmet logos

COMMUNICATIONS
To help reporters get their stories out, the NFL provides them with lots of help in the press box, such as special phones like this one from Super Bowl XX.

Former Raiders coach John Madden

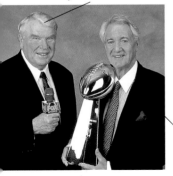

UP IN THE BOOTH
Super Bowl announcers usually include an expert analyst and a broadcaster who calls the play-by-play.

Veteran play-by-play man Pat Summerall

Super Stadiums

Tulane Stadium in New Orleans, on the campus of Tulane University, was the site of three Super Bowls, including IX.

THE GAME IS CERTAINLY SUPER, but why "Bowl"? That part of the Super Bowl's name comes from football stadiums, the earliest of which were shaped like deep bowls, such as the Yale Bowl in Connecticut. Important postseason college games began to be called "Bowls" after the shape of the stadium. So when it came time to name the NFL's championship game, the "Bowl" name just fit into football tradition. As for the Super Bowl stadiums themselves, 14 different stadiums hosted the first 34 Super Bowls. These ranged from indoor stadiums, such as the Superdome in New Orleans, to enormous open-air arenas, such as the Rose Bowl in Pasadena. Super Bowl stadiums are carefully prepared to be in tip-top condition for the big game. Not only are they decorated from top to bottom, new grass often is put on the field just before the game.

This fleet of buses in Miami for Super Bowl XIII helped nearly 80,000 people attend the game in the Orange Bowl.

BIG CROWDS
Every Super Bowl but the first one has been a sellout. The largest crowd ever to watch a Super Bowl was at Super Bowl XIV, when 103,985 people filled the Rose Bowl in Pasadena, California. Every Super Bowl stadium is ringed with hundreds of buses that bring fans from around the nation.

The roof of the Pontiac Silverdome is made of special heavy-duty fabric supported by rigid beams and air pressure.

Super Bowl stadium scoreboards keep fans entertained between plays and provide a wealth of information.

INDOOR ATTRACTION
The Pontiac Silverdome in Pontiac, Michigan, played host to Super Bowl XVI, including this college marching band during the pregame ceremonies. Nine Super Bowls have been played at four indoor stadiums: the Silverdome, the Louisiana Superdome, the Georgia Dome, and the Minneapolis Metrodome.

Circular ramps at Miami's Pro Player Stadium

SUPER CITIES
Miami and New Orleans each have hosted a record eight Super Bowls. Miami has had games at Pro Player Stadium (left), also known as Joe Robbie Stadium, as well as at the Orange Bowl. Miami was home to three of the first five games.

SUPER STADIUM SCENE

...is overhead view of the Rose Bowl in Pasadena, California,
...ring Super Bowl XXVII gives a spectacular panoramic
...w of Super Sunday. Although the game is held in January,
...ather rarely has been a big problem at the Super Bowl. The
...L mainly chooses cities with pleasant January weather,
...ich is appreciated by both players and fans.

*Blimps hover above every
outdoor Super Bowl stadium
to provide television viewers
with a birds-eye view.*

AN ENORMOUS TAILGATE PARTY

Before every Super Bowl, the NFL holds one of the
biggest tailgate parties in the world. Tailgate parties
are traditional pregame festivities held in the stadium
parking lot. At the Super Bowl, 20,000 people enjoy a
feast and great music before heading to the enty gates.

FANS GET IN THE ACT

At Super Bowl XXVII, the stadium was part of the
show. At halftime, singing star Michael Jackson put on
a showstopping performance. For part of the show,
the 98,374 people in the stands flipped colored cards
to create a stadium-spanning tableau of pictures of
children from around the world.

*Site of the "satellite city"
that TV networks from
around the world bring in to
broadcast the Super Bowl.*

*The Super Bowl stadium
end zones are specially
painted with team colors
of the participants.*

*The Rose Bowl has been the site
of five Super Bowls, and is
home to college football's oldest
postseason bowl game.*

*Crowds stream into the
stadium through a gauntlet of
souvenir stands, food stands,
and celebrating fans.*

Road to the Super Bowl

SUPER BOWL TEAMS are determined during the NFL playoffs, which begin the weekend after the regular season ends. Twelve teams earn playoff spots, six from the AFC and six from the NFC. The three division champions from each conference make the playoffs, while three wild-card teams (runner-up teams with best records) from each conference also reach the postseason. Following the wild-card playoffs are the divisional playoffs and then the conference championship games, with the winner advancing to the Super Bowl. The NFL playoffs often are among the most exciting games of the season…and the most important. Here are some of their stories.

Titans receiver Kevin Dyson had never before run the lateral play on which he scored.

WHO GOT IT?
A berth in Super Bowl XXX was determined on this play in the 1995 AFC Championship Game. If Colts receiver Aaron Bailey (in white) had made this catch, his team would have made the Super Bowl. Sadly for Colts fans, he didn't.

"THE MUSIC CITY MIRACLE"
In a 1999 wild-card playoff game, Tennessee trailed Buffalo 16-15 with only 16 seconds remaining. The Titans received the Bills' kickoff and ran a trick play called "Home Run Throwback." Lorenzo Neal fielded the ball and handed off to Frank Wycheck, who threw back across the field to Kevin Dyson (87), who ran 75 yards for a touchdown. It was one of the most amazing endings to a game in NFL history and helped boost the Titans to their first Super Bowl berth.

"THE DRIVE"
The Broncos trailed the Browns 20-13 with five minutes remaining in the 1986 AFC Championship Game. Then Denver quarterback John Elway led the Broncos on one of the greatest clutch marches in NFL playoff history. Elway ended the 98-yard drive with a touchdown pass to Mark Jackson with 37 seconds remaining to tie the score. In overtime, Rich Karlis (3), a barefoot kicker, nailed a 33-yard field goal that sent Denver to Super Bowl XXI.

HE GAVE IT ALL HE HAD
The San Diego Chargers' 41-38 overtime victory over Miami in the 1981 playoffs has been called one of the greatest games ever. The all-out effort of Chargers tight end Kellen Winslow (80) remains an inspiration.

Ball deflected backward

Harris catches at the X

Harris

"THE IMMACULATE RECEPTION"
This play from a 1972 AFC playoff game recently was voted the greatest play of the century by NFL fans. On the play, Pittsburgh's Franco Harris caught a pass that had been deflected backward, and Harris ran to the end zone to complete a 60-yard touchdown pass play to give the Steelers their first playoff win ever.

Disbelieving Raiders player gets the bad news.

COMEBACK!
Early in the third quarter of an 1992 AFC playoff game, the Buffalo Bills trailed the Houston Oilers 35-3. No problem: Bills quarterback Frank Reich (14) led Buffalo to the greatest comeback in playoff history— the Bills won 41-38 in overtime.

Handwarmer used in cold weather

George Halas Trophy for NFC championship

"THE CATCH"
San Francisco's Dwight Clark (87) prepares to spike the ball after his spectacular me-winning catch in the 1981 NFC Championship Game. The fingertip grab, on a 6-yard pass from Joe Montana, put the 49ers in their first Super Bowl.

ONE MORE TO PLAY
St. Louis quarterback Kurt Warner passed 30 yards to Ricky Proehl for a touchdown to clinch the Rams' 1999 NFC title. But while this trophy was nice, the Rams got the prize they really wanted by winning Super Bowl XXXIV.

Super Bowl XXXIV

WAS IT THE BEST SUPER BOWL EVER? You won't get much argument from the 72,625 fans who packed the Georgia Dome in Atlanta on January 30, 2000. They saw the climax of one of the NFL's greatest Cinderella stories when the St. Louis Rams defeated the Tennessee Titans 23-16 in a game that wasn't decided until the final play. The Rams came into the game as the improbable NFC champions, having gone from 3-13 in 1998 to 13-3 in 1999. They were led by Kurt Warner, a quarterback who literally had been bagging groceries only a few years before, and who had never started an NFL game before the '99 season. Warner led the Rams' passing attack, but early on, it was blunted by an equally determined Tennessee defense. The Rams led 9-0 at halftime.

Warner chose unifo... number 13 to sh... that he didn't belie... in bad lu...

THE SLIPPER F...
Kurt Warner beg... the 1999 season... the Rams' back... quarterback. ... ended it ... throwi... 2 touchdo... passes, settin... Super Bowl reco... with 414 passi... yards, and bei... named t... Super Bo... M...

BLOCK THAT KICK!
The Rams' Todd Lyght kept the Rams' lead at 9-0 with this block of a field-goal attempt by Tennessee's Al Del Greco early in the second half. Eight plays later the Rams scored to take a 16-0 lead.

Wood and cloth figure was more than 70 feet tall.

SHOWTIME!
Singing star Phil Collins is dwarfed by a giant statue that rose from the Georgia Dome floor during the halftime show. Collins was joined by a corps of dancers and an entire symphony orchestra.

GAME TIME
Steve McNair (9) charged onto the field during pregame introductions into a tunnel of teammates. McNair began the game as a somewhat unheralded player. He ended it as a part of Super Bowl history.

SIGNS OF THE TIME
Titans fans came to the game prepared to cheer on their heroes, including running back Eddie George. Although fans come to Super Bowls from around the country, the two teams bring the largest groups.

VALIANT EFFORT
Eddie George delivered a great performance in Super Bowl XXXIV. The Titans' running back ran for a game-high 95 yards and 2 touchdowns, helping lead Tennessee from behind to tie the Rams in the second half.

Some players wear protective rubber elbow sleeves on artificial turf.

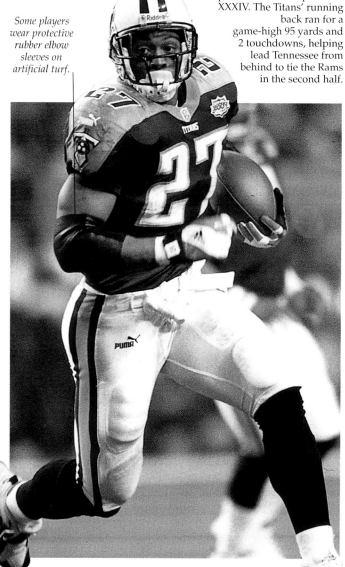

FIRST TOUCHDOWN
ms rookie receiver Torry Holt celebrates after scoring the first touchdown of he game. It came midway through the third quarter on a 9-yard pass from /arner. Holt bobbled the ball off his facemask before grabbing it to his chest for the touchdown. Teammate Isaac Bruce joins Holt in jumping for joy.

HOME SWEET DOME
The Georgia Dome, shown here during the pregame National Anthem performance, played host to its second Super Bowl. The first came in 1994 for Super Bowl XXVIII. The banners overhead featured legends of American music, the theme of the Super Bowl Pregame Show.

FIERY FANS
Why are these fans smiling? Their team is in the Super Bowl. From 1960-1996, the Titans played in Houston and were called the Oilers. The team moved to Tennessee in 1997, and changed its name to Titans in 1999. Titans are figures from Greek mythology; they were strong and powerful beings. One of the Titans, Prometheus, was said to have brought fire to mankind. So these Titans fans sport some fiery wigs—plus makeup in team colors—as they wait to enjoy Super Bowl XXXIV.

Super Bowl XXXIV

If the first half was quiet, the second half was another story. The Rams quickly added a touchdown to take a 16-0 lead. No team had ever come from that many points behind to win a Super Bowl. But Tennessee, led by the powerful running of Eddie George, rallied to tie the score with a little more than two minutes remaining, setting up the most exciting finish in Super Bowl history. First, Kurt Warner hit Isaac Bruce with a stunning 73-yard touchdown pass to retake the lead. Then Titans quarterback Steve McNair led his team back down the field. On the last play of the game, McNair passed to Kevin Dyson near the goal line. Dyson charged toward what would have been a tying touchdown…but the Rams' Mike Jones made a Super-Bowl-saving tackle!

SECOND TIME A CHARM
Rams coach Dick Vermeil led the Eagles to Super Bowl XV, but lost to Oakland. Older and wiser, he was a winner the second time around with St. Louis.

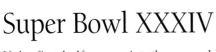

WHAT A PLAYER
In the final two minutes of Super Bowl XXXIV, Titans quarterback Steve McNair made play after play to keep his team in the game. Perhaps the greatest was when he barely eluded two Rams tacklers, nearly fell, then passed downfield for a key first down.

Special Super Bowl patch worn by all players

"THEY CAN PLAY "D", TOO"
The Rams led the NFL in scoring for the 1999 season, but their defense was overlooked. In the Super Bowl, Rams defenders such as Billy Jenkins made dozens of key plays.

The Rams were the first NFL team to wear logos or marks on their helmets, beginning in 1948.

BLUE AND GOLD
In 1995, the Rams moved from Los Angeles, where they had played since 1946, to St. Louis. These fans' sign proved to be prophetic.

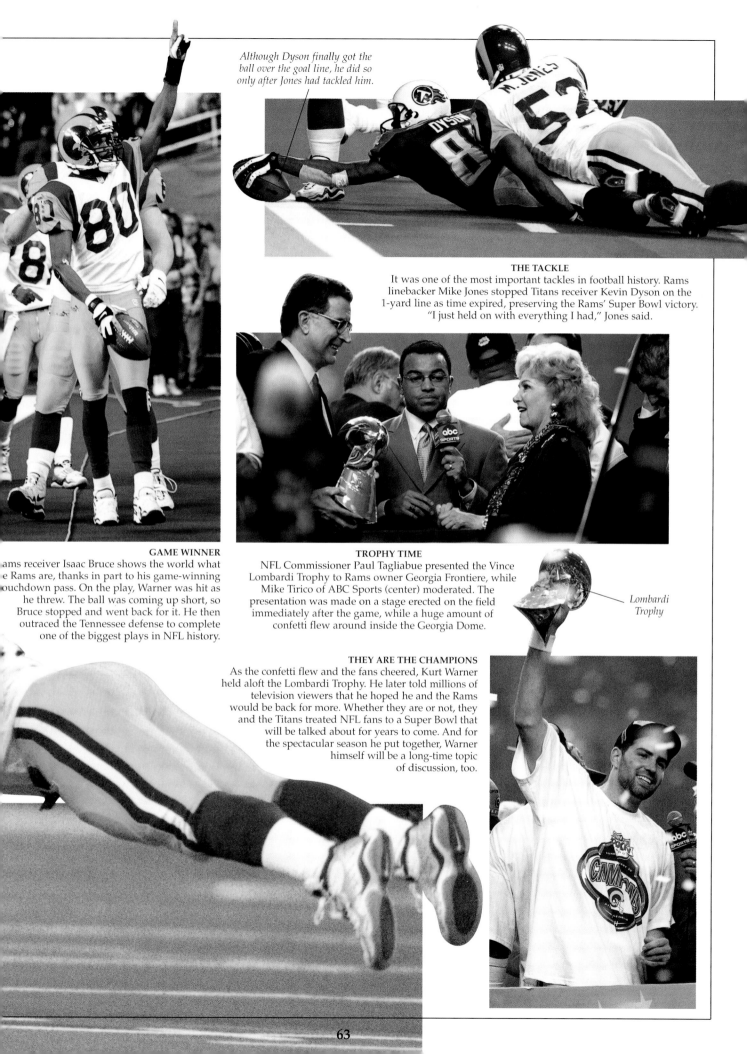

Although Dyson finally got the ball over the goal line, he did so only after Jones had tackled him.

THE TACKLE
It was one of the most important tackles in football history. Rams linebacker Mike Jones stopped Titans receiver Kevin Dyson on the 1-yard line as time expired, preserving the Rams' Super Bowl victory. "I just held on with everything I had," Jones said.

GAME WINNER
ams receiver Isaac Bruce shows the world what e Rams are, thanks in part to his game-winning ouchdown pass. On the play, Warner was hit as he threw. The ball was coming up short, so Bruce stopped and went back for it. He then outraced the Tennessee defense to complete one of the biggest plays in NFL history.

TROPHY TIME
NFL Commissioner Paul Tagliabue presented the Vince Lombardi Trophy to Rams owner Georgia Frontiere, while Mike Tirico of ABC Sports (center) moderated. The presentation was made on a stage erected on the field immediately after the game, while a huge amount of confetti flew around inside the Georgia Dome.

Lombardi Trophy

THEY ARE THE CHAMPIONS
As the confetti flew and the fans cheered, Kurt Warner held aloft the Lombardi Trophy. He later told millions of television viewers that he hoped he and the Rams would be back for more. Whether they are or not, they and the Titans treated NFL fans to a Super Bowl that will be talked about for years to come. And for the spectacular season he put together, Warner himself will be a long-time topic of discussion, too.

Index

---

www.nfl.com

Eyewitness Super Bowl was produced by the
Publishing Group of NFL Properties, Inc.

National Football League Properties, Inc.
Publishing Group
6701 Center Drive West, Suite 1111
Los Angeles, California 90045

NFL Publishing Staff:
Editor-in-Chief: John Wiebusch. General Manager: Bill Barron. Managing Editor: Chuck Garrity, Sr. Project
Editor: James Buckley, Jr. Project Art Director: Bill Madrid. Research: John Fawaz. Director-Photo Services:
Paul Spinelli. Photo Editor: Kevin Terrell. Manager-Photo Services: Tina Resnick. Director-Manufacturing:
Dick Falk. Director-Print Services: Tina Dahl. Manager-Computer Graphics: Sandra Gordon.
Publishing Director: Bob O'Keefe. Publishing Manager: Lori Quenneville.